INTERNATIONAL CHRISTIAN
GRADUATE UNIVERSITY

AUTHORITY IN THE CHURCH

A STUDY IN CHANGING PARADIGMS

by

T. Howland Sanks

Published by

American Academy of Religion

Dissertation Series, Number Two

Distributed by

SCHOLARS' PRESS
University of Montana
Missoula, Montana 59801

AUTHORITY IN THE CHURCH

A STUDY IN CHANGING PARADIGMS

by

T. Howland Sanks
College of the Holy Cross
Worcester, Massachusetts

Ph.D. 1971   Advisor:
University of Chicago   David Tracy

Copyright © 1974

by

American Academy of Religion

Library of Congress Catalog Card Number: 74-16565

ISBN: 0-88420-119-X

Printed in the United States of America

Printing Department

University of Montana

Missoula, Montana 59801

To Peg

PREFACE

This study arose from a concern for the malfunctioning of the teaching authority in the Roman Catholic church. That teaching authority has exerted great influence on the lives of the members of that communion and has been a major source for Roman Catholic theologians. It is an assumption of this thesis that there is a dialectical relationship between the life-experience of a community and the theoretical expression of that lived experience. More specifically in this instance, theology is both a product of the social experience of the Christian community and a factor in the construction of that experience.

This dissertation is confined to one half of that dialectical relation, namely, the theology of the magisterium, and does not explore the social reality of which that theology is a product and an articulation. It is hoped that an analysis of that theology and an understanding of the crisis in which it finds itself will contribute to a change in the social structure of the teaching authority in the Roman Catholic church. To that extent, this study is written not only for other theologians, but also for the bishops who currently exercise the teaching authority in the church.

My interest and research was stimulated and encouraged by my teachers both at Woodstock College and at the Divinity School of the University of Chicago and I wish to thank all of them, but especially David Tracy, my advisor, Langdon Gilkey, Martin Marty, Avery Dulles, and the late John Courtney Murray.

TABLE OF CONTENTS

CHAPTER I

INTRODUCTION

The Problem in the Current Situation

Until a few years ago the public image of the Roman
Catholic Church was that of a smoothly efficient authoritarian
monolith. That image was certainly exaggerated and perhaps
completely deceptive but it serves to put in relief the present
so-called crisis of authority in the Roman Catholic Church.
Some would prefer to call it a crisis of faith; others would
say that it merely reflects the breakdown of respect for authority in the society as a whole.

Two issues, I think, bring into focus the malfunctioning
of the teaching authority within the Roman Catholic Church
today--the publication and reaction to the encyclical Humanae
vitae in 1968 and, later, the dispute between the Dutch church
and the Vatican over priestly celibacy. In the first instance,
the pope promulgated a view on birth control that disagreed
with the recommendations of the majority of his own commission
and which had been a matter of public dispute among experts
for some time. Apparently the Vatican was surprised and unpre-
pared for the strong and widespread reaction to the encyclical.
In the United States a large group of theologians issued a
public statement the very day after the encyclical's release,
criticizing it strongly on several grounds.[1] In reaction, most
bishops in the U.S. seemed to feel that it was a question of
loyalty to the pope, and dealt with dissenters as "security

_____

[1]This statement and a discussion of the context may be
found in Charles E. Curran and Robert E. Hunt, Dissent In and
For the Church: Theologians and Humanae Vitae (New York:
Sheed & Ward, 1969), pp. 3-26. For a survey of other reactions,
see Richard J. McCormick, "Notes on Moral Theology," Theological Studies, XXX, No. 4 (December, 1969), 635-44.

risks."[1]

The discussion over priestly celibacy has not come to so clearcut a division, but the fact that there is public disagreement between the Dutch church, including their bishops, and the pope has instigated speculation about the possibility of schism once again. However unwarranted that may be, it is clear that there is some significant disagreement within the Roman Catholic church concerning the nature, status and function of the teaching authority, the magisterium. No less an authority than John Cardinal Heenan has described it as follows:

> Today what the pope says is by no means accepted as authoritative by all Catholic theologians. An article in the periodical Concilium is at least as likely to win their respect as a papal encyclical. The decline of the magisterium is one of the most significant developments in the post-Conciliar Church.[2]

The teaching authority of the church, the magisterium, has been generally understood until the recent crisis as the "perennial, authentic and infallible teaching office committed to the apostles by Christ and now possessed and exercised by their legitimate successors, the college of bishops in union with the pope."[3] The bishops at present understand themselves to be this authoritative teaching body, for they said in the Dogmatic Constitution on the Church of Vatican II, Lumen Gentium that "episcopal consecration, together with the office

---

[1]For example, in Washington, D.C., twenty priests were suspended from pastoral functions; in Baltimore, those who had signed the Theologians Statement were asked to write a letter affirming their loyalty to the pope; and in Buffalo, those who signed were dismissed from their teaching posts in the seminary.

[2]John Cardinal Heenan, "The Authority of the Church," The Tablet (London), 222 (May 18, 1968), 48.

[3]New Catholic Encyclopedia (New York: McGraw-Hill Book Co., 1967), p. 959. I use this only as a working definition with which to begin.

of sanctifying, also confers the offices of teaching and
governing."[1] This self-understanding of the bishops about how
they should exercise this perennial teaching office is of some
consequence in the current difficulties. Many factors contribute to this self-understanding (individual biographical
details, psychological state, the economic and cultural history
of the time, etc.) not least of which, however, was the theological education that these men have received. A large number of
bishops, especially in the United States, received their theological training at the Gregorian University.[2] After the closing
of many seminaries in Western Europe during the growth of the
secular state in the early part of the nineteenth century, more
and more of the clergy, particularly the episcopabiles, were
sent to Rome to newly-established national colleges. In time,
the Gregorian University came to serve as the primary academic
center for these colleges. Further, many professors in
seminaries elsewhere in the world were trained there. Six of
the last seven popes (including Pope Paul VI) studied there.
The theologians of the Gregorian faculty were very influential
from 1830 until 1959 for the reasons just given, but also
because of the success of ultramontane ideas within the church
and because of the intrinsic quality of their theological work.[3]
For example, when Newman wanted to study the official Catholic

[1]Walter M. Abbott, ed., Lumen Gentium, The Documents of
Vatican II (New York: The American Press, 1966), p. 41.

[2]The Liber Annualis of the Gregorian University for 1969
lists 230 American bishops as alumni (out of approximately 280)
and seven of the (then) ten cardinals. "The Greg," wrote LIFE
magazine, "is the Church's Oxbridge, Sorbonne and Yale-Harvard
all combined in one . . . the Crucible of Catholicism. It is
the university for any seminarian who aspires to prestige and
power in the Church." (European edition for July 7, 1969).

[3]Roger Aubert, "La Geographie Ecclésiologique au XIXe
siècle," "L'Ecclésiologie au XIXe siècle," Unam Sanctam, XXXIV
(Paris: Les Editions de Cerf, 1960), 36 ff.

theology after his conversion, he went to Rome (1846-47) and
reported that the only theologians there were the Jesuits (at
the Gregorian), Giovanni Perrone, Carlo Passaglia, and Clemens
Schrader.[1] The doctrine of the magisterium as it was taught
at the Gregorian University during the period between the
Vatican Councils was significant, then, for these reasons: it
was the theology "in possession," the official theology of the
Roman Catholic church during this period, and the theology in
which a large number of the current members of the episcopal
magisterium were trained. It is a major source of the current
understanding of the nature and function of the magisterium as
well as of the current dispute about that function. For as
long as there are people trained in this theology of the magisterium active in the life of the church, it will effect the
form and function of that teaching authority.

It is clear, I think, that the theologians who disagree
with and criticize Humanae vitae have a different view of the
nature and function of the magisterium than do the pope or
many of the bishops. This disagreement does not seem to be
based principally in diverging exegetical views of Scripture or
the Fathers nor even on a dispute among historians. Although it
is true that the renewal of biblical, patristic and historical
studies has led to new insights and emphases in ecclesiology,
these studies have also made us aware of the hermeneutical
difficulties involved and of the presuppositions a scholar
brings to a text or a body of material. The criticism of the
theologians concerning Humanae vitae was not based on the papal
use of Scripture, the Fathers or other monumenta Christiana--

---

[1]Owen Chadwick, From Bossuet to Newman (Cambridge: The
University Press, 1957), p. 167.

the usual theological data. Rather, the encyclical is taken to task for its implied ecclesiology, the methodology employed in its writing and promulgation, its "narrow and positivistic notion of papal authority," an inadequate concept of natural law, and its "static worldview", among other things.[1] To understand the current crisis, then, it would seem that we must look beyond the theological data to the fundamental presuppositions operative in the diverse views of the nature and function of the magisterium.

Sources and Methodology

In order to understand this crisis of the nature and function of the magisterium in the Roman Catholic church, I have employed as a heuristic device the theory of paradigm-change advanced by Thomas S. Kuhn on the basis of his study of the history of scientific discoveries.[2] Kuhn's notion of paradigms and of the crisis that occurs in a discipline when those paradigms are no longer shared by a significant minority of that community is a means of discovering and articulating the presuppositions of a particular body of knowledge, in this case the theology of the Roman School. Kuhn uses the word "paradigm" somewhat vaguely and I will discuss this in greater detail in Chapters IV and V, but basically it is the model or exemplar, whether concrete or conceptual on the basis of which data are organized and interpreted, questions asked and methods of solutions proposed.

Kuhn's theory, of course, can only be applied analogously

---

[1] Curran and Hunt, Dissent In and For the Church, pp. 25-26.

[2] Thomas S. Kuhn, The Structure of Scientific Revolutions (Chicago: The University of Chicago Press, 1970).

to the theological world. There are obvious differences between theology and the natural sciences of physics and chemistry, from which Kuhn takes most of his examples. Theological models cannot be quantified, nor are they the basis of repetitive problem-solving. There are, however, models operative in theology, both in the broader sense of the constellation of shared beliefs, values, and techniques of the community, as well as the more specific sense of models or exemplars on the basis of which a number of questions are approached. In the case of the doctrine of the magisterium, there are both paradigms specific to this doctrine and paradigms that underly the entire theological system of which this doctrine is only a small part. The act-potency model in traditional scholastic theology, on the basis of which the sacraments, faith, the virtues, the Incarnation, etc., are analyzed, is a good example of the latter. When it comes to the teaching authority of the church, there are models of teaching, of truth, of authority, and of the socio-political structure of the church. Sometimes they are explicated and sometimes not, and I am not suggesting that they were consciously adopted as such by the theologians in question.

That there is an ideological component to all knowledge has been well enough established and there is no need to argue it here. It is necessary, however, as Gregory Baum points out,

> . . . for each branch of knowledge to make explicit the hidden presupposition operative in it . . . and institute a systematic critique of these presuppositions from its own point of view as well as submit to the critique offered by other branches of knowledge. This sort of inquiry sets up a self-corrective process by which knowledge successively abandons bias and prejudices, frees itself from its ideological component, and reaches out for results that are acceptable to even wider groups of people living under diverse social conditions--without however trying to give up the values that are constitutive of its essential task.[1]

_____

[1]Gregory Baum, "Theology and Ideology," The Ecumenist, January-February, 1970, p. 25.

This is all the more necessary for theology whose purpose is to serve the Gospel and hence must make the effort to "reach out to ever wider groups of people living under diverse social conditions."

There are several reasons why I think Kuhn's theory is helpful in discovering and analyzing the presuppositions of the theology of the magisterium and the current disagreement about it. First of all, Kuhn's description of the process of revolution in science evokes a striking similarity to the present situation in Roman Catholic theology with regard to the nature and function of the magisterium. It seems, as I have said, to be a matter, not of new data, nor merely of reinterpretation, but of a basically different way of looking at the theological "world". Kuhn, with some qualifications, compares it to a gestalt shift. The two issues I mentioned earlier (the disagreements about birth control and priestly celibacy) suggest something as basic as that. Secondly, Kuhn himself suggests the comparison with theology as the discipline most similar to science, insofar as textbooks are the major authoritative source for the communication of information, vocabulary, syntax and the paradigms of the community of practitioners.[1] This domination of "mature science" by texts was true of Roman Catholic theology during the period between the Vatican Councils, and was especially true of the Roman School. Thirdly, I believe, with Kuhn, that "the search for assumptions (even for non-existent ones) can be an effective way to weaken the grip of a tradition upon the mind and to suggest the basis for a new one."[2] If that can be done in the case of the theology

---

[1] Kuhn, _The Structure of Scientific Revolutions_, pp. 136-37, 166.

[2] _Ibid._, p. 88.

of the magisterium of the Roman School we may make some
contribution toward easing the crisis.

Further, Kuhn's theory that major changes in the way a
scientific community views the world are due to shifts in the
basic paradigms of that community may contribute to an understanding of one of the problems with the magisterium that has
persisted in Catholic theology throughout the period we are
treating--that of the "development of dogma." One of the major
reasons (e.g., in the Minority Report of the Papal Commission)
for not changing the Roman Catholic church's teaching on birth
control was that it was unthinkable that the church could have
been wrong about such an important matter involving "faith and
morals" for so long.[1] This problem of change in the authoritative teaching of the church was in the background during
Vatican II and still looms as one of the major anomalies in the
current Roman Catholic crisis. After we have analyzed the
doctrine of the magisterium of the Roman School in terms of
Kuhn's theory, we will be in a position to elaborate further on
its implications for a more general theory of development.

Since, according to Kuhn and as a matter of empirical fact
in the case of the faculty of the Gregorian University during
this period, the paradigms are transmitted through textbooks, I
have confined my exposition and analysis to the texts which
these men have published. Their classroom notes became their
textbooks and are a faithful representation of what they thought
and what the students were taught.[2] Although a number of the

---

[1]Daniel Callahan, ed., The Catholic Case for Contraception
(New York: The Macmillan Company, 1969), pp. 187-88, 209-10.

[2]Kuhn, The Structure of Scientific Revolutions, pp. 10 and
166. Until the latter part of the period textbooks were their
only vehicle.

texts went through several editions, there were not significant changes and when these have occurred, I have noted them. Further, since the study is not primarily a textual one, I have used the editions available in this country. I am primarily interested in the content and presuppositions of their doctrine of the magisterium.

Despite some individual differences which I have noted in the course of the thesis, the teaching on the magisterium of all these men was similar enough to warrant treating them as a "school". One man trained the next in most cases, and Walter Kasper and C. G. Arevalo, who have done studies of the early period, agree in calling them a "school."[1] They constantly cite one another and all the later figures operate in the context of Franzelin's classic work. They are truly a "community of practitioners." Hence, I have not done a study of the complete theology of each man, but rather of one doctrine taught by one school. Further, it is beyond the scope of my study to trace the cultural influences on the paradigms involved or the psychological sources in each man. Important as these are, that would require a separate study. While it is one of the assumptions of the thesis that the social reality and its symbolic expression in theology are mutually related, I have explored only the symbolic expression.[2]

By examining the Kalendaria of the Gregorian University

---

[1] Walter Kasper, Die Lehre von der Tradition in der Römischen Schule (Freiburg: Herder, 1962), passim; and C. G. Arévalo, "Some Aspects of the Theology of the Mystical Body of Christ in the Ecclesiology of Giovanni Perrone, Carlo Passaglia and Clemens Schrader," (Unpublished doctoral dissertation, Gregorian University, 1959).

[2] The theoretical expression of this assumption may be found in Peter L. Berger and Thomas Luckmann, The Social Construction of Reality (New York: Doubleday & Company, Inc., Anchor Books edition, 1967).

for this period one can determine who taught the theology of the
magisterium at any given time. These were the men whose texts
I have investigated: John Baptist Cardinal Franzelin, who
taught there from 1858 to 1876 but whose work is the most significant and became the framework for the theology of the magisterium of his successors; Domenicus Palmieri (1869-1879);
Camillo Cardinal Mazzella (1878-1885); Louis Cardinal Billot
(1885-1910) who is the second most outstanding theological
figure but more for his work in other areas of dogmatic theology; Hermann Van Laak (1901-1916 and 1920-1928) whose teaching
career there was long but undistinguished; and finally, Timotheus Zapelena (1929-1959). One familiar with pre-Vatican II
ecclesiology might wonder why the name of Sebastian Tromp, well-
known for his work on the Mystical Body theology, is not included.[1] Tromp's tenure at the Gregorian University coincided with
that of Zapelena, (1930-1958), but they so divided the subject-
matter of ecclesiology that Tromp did not treat the doctrine of
the magisterium.

Not all of these men are equally important and much of
their work is repetitious, so, while I have examined all the
pertinent material, I have not presented them all in the same
detail. I trust the presentation is sufficient to warrant the
paradigm analysis that follows.

Although the Roman School began before Vatican I, I have
used the two councils as landmarks rather than as exact termini
for the period. I have treated briefly the "founding fathers"

---

[1]It is generally accepted in Rome that Tromp was at least
the main source if not the actual author of Pius XII's encycli-
cal, Mystici corporis (1943). He was a consultor to the Holy
Office from 1950 on and a peritus at the Second Vatican Council.
He is best known for his Corpus Christi quod est Ecclesia (Rome:
The Gregorian University Press, 1946), English translation by
Ann Condit (New York: Vantage Press, 1960).

of the Roman School--Giovanni Perrone, Carlo Passaglia and
Clemens Schrader--but have not dealt specifically with the
documents of Vatican I since they are the products of the theology of the Roman School rather than its source.

Historical Background

As theological treatises go, ecclesiology is perhaps the
youngest member of the family. "The Oldest Treatise on the
Church" is a title given to James of Viterbo's De regimine
christiano which appeared in 1301 or 1302. It and several
others of the time were occasioned by the conflict between
Philip the Fair and Boniface VIII. Since that time the treatise
on the church has developed out of similar contexts of con-
flict--with conciliarism, Gallicanism, Protestantism, the
secularism of the state and Modernism. It has been built, as
Congar remarks, like the Temple after the Exile, "With sword in
hand!"

As an aspect of ecclesiology, the theology of the magisterium has shared these characteristics, and to an even more
marked degree. It did not receive individual treatment as such
until the period we are studying. As late as 1946, the Dictionnaire Théologie Catholique has no entry under that title. There
is no published history of the doctrine of the magisterium. But
neither is there any doubt that there has always been some form
of authoritative teaching in the church. A brief survey of its
development, basically through the eyes of Congar, will provide
some perspective for my own study.

Based on Christ's injunction to "Go forth and teach all
nations whatever I have commanded you," (Mt 28:18ff) and his
promise of the Spirit of Truth (Jn 16:12ff), the Apostles taught
others and commissioned others to teach also. Teaching was one

of the offices or ministries listed in the early church (I Cor

12:28-31; Rom 12:6-8; Eph 4:11). The Apostles' teaching was

authoritative because of their close association with the Lord,

and Paul also claims this authority but on the basis of gifts he

has received (I Cor 7:10, 12, 17) and speaks of authority as

service for Jesus' sake (II Cor 4:5; I Cor 9:19) rather than in

terms of "domineering" over the faithful as lords and masters.[1]

"The highest authority in the community was reserved to the

apostles, or to such trusted collaborators as Timothy or Titus

(I Tim 3:1-15; 5:22; Tit 1:5) and others who emerged as founders

of congregations and apostolic envoys all of whom derived their

authority directly from the apostles."[2] The present-day divis-

ion of offices into bishops, priests, and deacons developed only

later as the church took on a more definite form and the role of

officers received greater importance. It is first mentioned by

Ignatius of Antioch.[3] The more important point as far as the

early church is concerned is the following fact: "that the

ministers had authority to teach the faithful in continuity

with the apostles is found, in one form or another, in all the

ancient documents."[4]

How authoritative teaching came to be bound up with the

hierarchical offices in the church is not altogether clear, but

Congar accepts C. H. Turner's explanation that it was in re-

sponse to the Gnostic challenge that the Catholics affirmed the

---

[1]Yves M.-J. Congar, "The Historical Development of Authority," in Problems of Authority, ed. by John M. Todd (Baltimore:
The Helicon Press, 1962), p. 120 ff.

[2]Hans Küng, Structures of the Church, trans. by Salvator
Attanasio (New York: Thomas Nelson & Sons, 1964), pp. 207-08.

[3]Hans Küng, Structures of the Church, pp. 207-08.

[4]Yves M.-J. Congar, Tradition and Traditions (New York:
The Macmillan Company, 1966), pp. 35-36; Damien Van den Eynde,
Les Normes de l'enseignement chrétien dans la littérature pa-
tristique des trois premier siècles (Paris, 1933), pp. 57-67.

13

bond between the true traditions and the succession of legitimate ministers, bishops or presbyters, from the apostles. Thus
the idea of succession became the guarantee of authentic interpretation.[1]

In the period from the apostles until Constantine, authority in the church (not just teaching authority) developed with
three features: "a strong insistence on authority, a very close
link with the Christian community, and a marked charismatic
or spiritual character."[2] Ignatius of Antioch, Irenaeus,
Hippolytus, Origen and Cyrpian all emphasize authority strongly.
But this authority is closely related to the community--in
making decisions, in electing bishops, for example--and it is
Cyprian who says that the "bishop is in the Church and the
Church is in the bishop."[3] The bishop was also the man possessed of the most charismatic or spiritual gifts. He was chosen as
a man endowed with the Spirit. The Spirit was not confined to
the office of bishop, but it was expected that it be joined to
the office.[4]

With the establishment of the church in Constantine's
reign, the bishops became public men of rank, administrators
of justice, defenders of the poor, widows, etc. The authority
in the church became more secular and juridical and tended to
become authority for its own sake. The more charismatic or
spiritual elements were kept alive by the growth of monasticism.
Spiritual authority was separated to some extent from the hierarchical structure and the "men of God" had an authority that

[1]Congar, Tradition and Traditions, p. 36.

[2]Congar, "The Historical Development of Authority," p. 124.

[3]Ibid., p. 125.

[4]Ibid., p. 127.

was almost autonomous. The startsi in Russia were a lasting
example of this kind of phenomenon. Authoritative teaching,
then, could be found in people who had no particular office in
the structure of the church. Congar reminds us, however, that
"it would be a mistake to see any opposition between this type
of authority and that exercised by the bishops," for many of the
bishops were monks or had had monastic training, and the bishop,
whether a monk or not, was a man of God and had spiritual obli-
gations.[1] What is clear, however, is that teaching with authority about the word of God was not restricted to any one office
in the ecclesiastical structure.

Congar suggests that there was a decisive turning point in
the twelfth century at the time of the Gregorian Reform (Gregory
VII, 1073-1081)--"a transition from an appreciation of the ever-
active presence of God to that of juridical powers put at the
free disposal of, and perhaps even handed over as its property
to, 'the Church,' i.e., the hierarchy." There was a shift from
the notion that ecclesiastical structures were the manifestation
and form of God's action, a manifestation of the invisible in
the visible, to a "process of translation or construction of the
Christian realities in terms of form or nature and of causality,
within the scholastic context, with its 'physicism' and its
ontology." Before this time the action of God is not seen as
totally committed to regular structures of the Church, i.e., it
"allows for the possibility of the unforeseen intervention of
God or his Spirit. There are the theses on the salvation of
non-Catholics, on unjust excommuncation, on the freedom of the
Holy Spirit . . ."[2] But from this time on, a more juridical
paradigm of authority (including the teaching authority)

---

[1]Congar, "The Historical Development of Authority," p.130.
[2]Congar, Tradition and Traditions, p. 135.

prevails. Those in the structured offices in the church,
especially the pope, came to be seen as possessing God's
authority rather than as imperfectly reflecting it through
delegation.[1]

The Gregorian Reform attempted to free the church from
its identification with the political society and its domination
by laymen. To this end, "Gregory claimed for the church the
completely autonomous and sovereign system of rights proper to
a spiritual society. . . . To support his claims, he had asked
churchmen (Peter Damien to begin with) to discover the maximum
number of juridical texts in favour of this view."[2] Thus began
the real science of Canon Law, and this development led to the
juridical interpretation of many scriptual texts that had,
heretofore, been interpreted in a more spiritual sense (Congar
gives the examples of Jer 1:10, I Cor 2:15 and 6:3, I Pet 2:9
and Lk 10:16). The overall result as far as the notion of the
magisterium is concerned was that a doctrine had authority because it was enunciated by those who had a legal title to the
power handed on from the past, rather than because of the in-
herent truth of the doctrine. This tendency, although it had
its beginnings in the twelfth century came to full force in
response to the challenge of the Reformation.

We might note, before we pass to the Tridentine reaction,
that among St. Thomas and his contemporaries "magisterium"
designates the function of professors rather than of the hierarchy. It was a scholarly magisterium based on the free
exchange of ideas in the university. The notion of magisterium
had not yet been confined to the juridical model whose origins

[1]A. Weiler, "Church Authority and Government in the Middle
Ages," Concilium, VII (Glen Rock: Paulist Press, 1965), 131.

[2]Congar, "The Historical Development of Authority," pp.
136-39.

we have just discussed.[1]

The challenge to authority posed by the Reformers was a very basic one since it was not just a questioning of authority in the historical form then existing, but a challenge to ecclesiastical authority in principle. Luther started out more concerned with the content of the Gospel, the _quod_ but after the confrontation with Cardinal Cajetan (Augsburg, October, 1518) the formal principle of the Reformation, the _quo_, that everything must be judged by the criterion of Scripture alone, dominated. Far more than the principle of justification by faith, which could be interpreted in a sense acceptable to the Roman Catholics, the challenge to the authority of the popes and councils threatened the very existence of the Catholic church. The church's reaction "consisted in the twofold process which the church normally brings into operation when she is seriously challenged. On the one hand, she reasserted her authority and gave it a greater degree of centralization. On the other hand, she revised the idea and the practice of authority on the moral and pastoral planes."[2]

With the loss of unanimity on tradition, the emphasis in the post-Reformation period shifts from the "objective magisterium"--i.e., tradition objectively considered--to a magisterium of authority, the active magisterium of the present rather than the content of the ancient deposit.

> This theology is characterized by the affirmation
> of the principle of authority, that is to say the
> formal principle or _quo_, in a way which hardly
> allows for its conditioning by the content, the

---

[1]Avery Dulles, "The Magisterium in Contemporary Focus," _Theology Digest_, XVII, 4 (Winter, 1969), 301; Congar, "The Historical Development of Authority," p. 145, n. 3.

[2]Congar, "The Historical Development of Authority," p. 144.

objective datum or quod: authority in so far as
it actually is authority, in other words, the
exact opposite of the position taken up by the
Reformers.[1]

Since the sixteenth century, Congar says, the Catholic church

has practiced a veritable "mystique" of authority which may be

characterized as "the notion of a complete identification of

God's will with the institutional form of authority. In the

latter, it is God himself whose voice we hear and heed."

Obedience becomes the fundamental virtue[2] and the characteristic

text is "Who hears you, hears me," (Lk 10:16).

Trent itself did not even use the word "magisterium" and

the Council was concerned mainly to defend the existence of

apostolic traditions in opposition to the Reformers insistence

on sola Scriptura. But this defense and its implications, com-

bined with the challenge to ecclesiastical authority, led to

questions about theological criteria, theological sources and

the rule of faith. Once these questions were raised in a

juridical manner, as Congar remarks, "it was inevitable that

tradition should be identified with the magisterium."[3] This

tendency reached its fullness in the theologians we will be

studying, but it was foreshadowed in the eighteenth century by

the French Dominican Billuart, who made tradition a rule of

faith only insofar as it had been proposed by the magisterium.[4]

One other notion that contributed to this development,

---

[1]Congar, Tradition and Traditions, p. 176.

[2]In the structure of the Society of Jesus, for example,
and in the bull which condemned Luther, Exsurge, we read:
Nervus ecclesiasticae disciplinae, obedientiam scilicet, quae
fons est et origo omnium virtutum, (Mansi, XXXII, col. 1053).

[3]Congar, Tradition and Traditions, p. 181.

[4]Charles Rene Billuart, O. P. (1685-1757), Cursus Theologiae, Tract. De Regulis Fidei, Diss. II, a. 1; also A. Michel,
"Tradition," D.T.C., XV, col. 1328 ff.

which became a main thesis of the Tübingen School, and through
Perrone's reading of Möhler influenced the Roman School, was the
idea of "living tradition." This notion had had its origin with
the Catholic adversaries of the Reformers, to counter the emphasis on the verbum scriptum with the theme of the "Gospel written
in men's hearts." The idea was employed again in the controversy with the Jansenists who said that theology was confined
to what was expressly stated in its sources. Against this, the
notion of a "'living tradition' or 'the common and present
teaching' of the Church," was urged. This idea passed through
Fenelon to Sailer, Drey and then to Möhler and the Catholic
school at Tübingen.[1] For Möhler, "living tradition" is not the
magisterium but the "Gospel written in men's hearts." The Holy
Spirit animates all the faithful, in his organic view of the
church, and it is "This vital, spiritual force, which we
inherit from our fathers and which is perpetuated in the church,
(which) is interior tradition."[2] This more organic, vitalistic
approach to ecclesiology was one of the factors contributing to
the interest in the Mystical Body image among the early members
of the Roman School, as we will see.

The theologians of the Roman School were in continuity
with this historical tendency toward authoritarianism and
juridicism. The Mystical Body theology, which would have provided some corrective balance and which almost came to birth in
the Tübingen School and the early members of the Roman School
was aborted by two historical events. The fact that the First
Vatican Council was never able to discuss the De ecclesia

---

[1]See Congar, Tradition and Traditions, pp. 186-191, for
fuller discussion and bibliography.

[2]J. A. Möhler, Die Einheit, par. 3, as quoted by Congar,
Tradition and Traditions, p. 194.

schema nor to complete its treatment of the hierarchical structure, and the fallout that ensued, led ecclesiologists once again to rise to the defense of the papal power. There was still a preoccupation with authority in the church in response to the secularism and autonomy of the state in France, Italy and Germany, as well as in response to the challenge to authority posed by the growth of historical studies. There was also a revival of what Aubert calls "neo-ultra-montanism" in both France and England.[1] The French felt a greater need for identification with Rome after the secularism of the Third Republic, and the increasing self-awareness of Catholics in England in the wake of the Oxford Movement led them in the same direction. We are all familiar with W. G. Ward's desire to have a papal bull delivered every morning with the newspaper! In Germany, the condemnation of Döllinger and the defection of the Old Catholics made theologians cautious about any theories that would seem not to give sufficient stress to the position of the hierarchy and especially that of the pope.

The second major factor in retarding the development of a more balanced ecclesiology was the Modernist crisis. Although not explicitly an ecclesiological battle, it was seen as a challenge to the authority of the church and raised questions basic to theological method and to an understanding of the church, before the time was ripe. In an attempt to respond to Harnack, Loisy published in 1902 his L'Evangile et L'Eglise in which he proposed a theory of development of dogma that did not seem, to the Roman authorities and theologians at least, to preserve the truth of revelation sufficiently. It was said that Loisy and Tyrell (although there were others such as Von Hügel,

---

[1]Aubert, "La Geographie Ecclésiologique as XIXe Siècle," passim.

Murri and Fogazzaro) were striking not at one dogma but at the very basis of a rational and knowable structure of doctrine. Billot, the Gregorian theologian, in responding to them considered Loisy's theory pure relativism and attacked him strongly in his De Immutabilitate Traditionis contra modernam haeresim evolutionismi (1904). The harshness of the official response of the pope in the decree Lamentabili and the encyclical Pascendi gregis (1907) discouraged the pursuit of any theological questions that might threaten or seem to threaten the authority centralized in Rome.

Even when the renewal of ecclesiology began between the two World Wars under the influence of the liturgical movement, the ecumenical movement, the renewal of Catholic biblical and patristic studies and the growth of a theology of the laity, the doctrine of the magisterium was not affected. The juridical model that had dominated the treatment of the magisterium was not integrated with the newer Mystical Body model, as we will see. Thus crisis in the church concerning the nature and function of the magisterium had its beginning in the period we shall discuss and before. It is the thesis of this study that it is not yet resolved. I hope that the succeeding pages will contribute to an understanding of its present status.

CHAPTER II

THE THEOLOGY OF THE MAGISTERIUM AT THE

GREGORIAN UNIVERSITY -- EARLY PERIOD

Theological Background

Franzelin's doctrine of tradition (in which is included
his treatment of the magisterium) is like the ripe fruit of the
theological endeavors of Perrone, Passaglia and Schrader, says
Walter Kasper.[1] They were the founders of the "Roman School"
and the predecessors of the men with whom we are concerned.
The doctrine of the magisterium of the Gregorian professors
has its theological roots in the ecclesiology of these three
men. They were the teachers and colleagues of Franzelin.

Their ecclesiology and their doctrine of tradition has
been thoroughly treated by Heribert Schauf and Walter Kasper
and by Catalino Arévalo in an unpublished dissertation.[2] It is
not necessary to duplicate their excellent studies here, but
a brief summary of the theology of Perrone, Passagalia and
Schrader is necessary to situate the doctrine of the magisterium as it was presented at the Gregorian University by
their successors.

Giovanni Perrone

When Pope Leo XII restored the Roman College to the

_____

[1]Kasper, Die Lehre von der Tradition in der Römischen
Schule, p. 4.

[2]Heribert Schauf, Carl Passaglia und Clemens Schrader,
Beitrag zur Theologiegeschichte des neunzehnten Jahrhundrets
(Rome: Pontificia Universitas Gregoriana, 1938), Die Einwoh-
nung des Heiligen Geistes (Freiburg/Br.: Herder, 1941), De
Corpore Christi Mystico sive de Ecclesia Christi theses: Die
Ekklesiologie des Konzilstheologen Clemens Schrader, S.J.
(Freiburg: Herder, 1959), Walter Kasper, Die Lehre von der
Tradition in der Römischen Schule, C. G. Arévalo, "Some Aspects
of the Theology of the Mystical Body of Christ in the Eccle-
siology of Giovanni Perrone, Carlo Passaglia and Clemens
Schrader."

Society of Jesus in 1824, Giovanni Perrone was among the first
group of professors and soon became the Prefect of Studies.
Born in Chieri near Turin in 1794, he entered the Jesuits in
1815, studied at the major seminary at Turin and received the
doctorate in theology there. Except for four years when he was
rector at Ferrara (1830-34) and the two years when the Jesuits
left Rome because of the political situation (1848-50), his
entire theological career was spent at the Roman College. His
reputationwas world-wide, however, and his influence great.
Indeed, Hocedez says that he was "the best-known theologian
of his age."[1] He had great respect for and knowledge of the
Christian tradition as well as familiarity with the contemporary theologians of his time, both Catholics and Protestants.
He was particularly influenced by Mohler.[2] He was on a number
of Roman Congregations and a member of the commissions which
prepared the definition of the dogma of the Immaculate Conception and prepared for the First Vatican Council. Pius IX had
particular regard for him and wanted to make him a cardinal
but Perrone refused. Newman sought him out when he was in Rome,
and these two though they disagreed and had basically diverse
orientations, respected one another and engaged in serious
discussion.[3]

---

[1]Edgar Hocedez, Histoire de la Théologie au XIXe Siècle
(3 vols.; Paris: Desclée de Bouwer, 1947-52), II, 253.

[2]Arevalo gives a table of Perrone's citations of Mohler
on pp. 62-65, but the overall influence of Möhler on the Roman
School is a matter of some dispute, cf. Kasper, Die Lehre von
der Tradition in der Römischen Schule, pp. 7 ff.

[3]Owen Chadwick, From Boussuet to Newman (Cambridge, Eng.:
Cambridge University Press, 1957), pp. 166-84, cf. also chapter
V, Newman;   T. Lynch, "The Newman-Perrone Paper on Develop-
ment," Gregorianum, XVI (1935), 402-47.

Although he may not have been very original, he was clear
and precise--so much so that Newman and Ambrose St.
John "judged his thought to be 'cut-and-dried',"[1]--and this contributed to the wide use of his books, most influential of
which were the Praelectiones theologicae dogmaticae, which up
to 1888 had gone through thirty-four editions, and the shorter
version of these, the Compendium, which had forty-seven editions up to 1892. These were written to combat the errors of
the time, the principle one being, for Perrone, the autonomy of
Reason, or rationalism.[2] This, as well as the desire to res-
tore unity and order, (which Kasper suggests is the general
mentality of the "Restoration" period reacting against the
overemphasis on freedom and individuality),[3] is reflected in
Perrone's doctrine of the church and of the magisterium.

Citing Möhler, Perrone says that the church is like
Christ--as a society it is the visible continuation of the
Incarnation. Like Christ, it is divine-human; the two are
closely interrelated but the divine "pervades and penetrates"
the human, rules and directs it.[4] In this "moral person"
the divine is the "soul" and the human is the exterior form or
"body," and consequently, the church is both invisible and
visible. It has qualities like Christ: the church is one as
Christ is one, the church is holy as Christ is holy, the church

---

[1]Ibid., p. 180.

[2]Rationalism, for Perrone, is that system according to
which there is no other revelation except that given through
human reason. Its origin is to be sought in Kantian philosophy
and had such followers in Germany as Fichte, Koppen, Niethammer,
Grohmann and Nitzch. Giovanni Perrone, Praelectiones Theologicae, (4 vols. revised edition Paris: Guame Fratres,
1856), I, 2, n. 2. (Hereinafter referred to simply as
Praelectiones.)

[3]Kasper, Die Lehre von der Tradition in der Römischen
Schule, p. 53.

[4]Perrone, Praelectiones, IV, 19, nos. 44 ff.

24

is indefectible as Christ is indefectible, the church is infallible as Christ is infallible. Christ is head of the church
perpetually and has an indissoluble bond with his spouse, the
faithful.[1]

This idea of the church as the continuation of the Incarnation with the same qualities as Christ himself underlies
Perrone's view that the church is not only a mediator of the
Word of God to men, but is the immediate direct witness of the
Word of God. The doctrine and practice of the church is the
immediate, direct, representation of divine tradition.[2] The
church has the divine tradition directly from God. The Scripture has to be read and understood in the church; its whole
power comes from the witness of the church.[3] Thus, there is
strong emphasis on the authoritative teaching of the church.

The foundation of this teaching authority for Perrone
is that Christ left the deposit of faith (integrum fidei
depositum) to the apostles under the primacy of Peter and his
successors and commanded them to teach all nations, bringing
them to the faith. Christ further promised to be with them all
days (Mt 28:18ff). While some of this deposit was written down
by the apostles, the rest was carried viva voce, and this
latter determines the sense of what was written down and com-
pletes it.[4] Thus the mission of Christ is continued in the
mission of the apostles, and this was intended by Christ to go
on in space and time until the end of time. Kasper points out
that this is explained by Perrone with the aid of two basic
notions--that of "representation" and that of "moral person."

---

[1]Ibid., 194.

[2]Kasper, Die Lehre von der Tradition in der Römischen
Schule, p. 53.

[3]Ibid., p. 80.
[4]Perrone, Praelectiones, IV, 502.

"Moral person," or "moral body" for Perrone, is a group of
people who act and operate like a man or an individual living
person. It has a "vital principle" or "soul" by which the mass
is moved and through which it exercises its powers; it has an
"exterior form" or "body," and the two are intimately and
mutually related.[1] In the apostles Christ has formed a "moral
person" which is a continuation of himself, and this body re-
presents the whole teaching church. Their successors continue
this "moral person" and take possession of and preserve the
teaching given in the original "deposit."[2] The bishops as the
heirs and successors of the apostles form, all together, a
moral unity. Only this "living and perpetual magisterium" is
adequate for knowing the doctrine divinely handed down.[3] It is
not the "dead voice of a codex of manuscripts but the living
and public voice of the church that is always the first and
proximate rule of faith."[4] Thus, as Kasper points out, there
is a devaluation of the regulae fidei remotae (i.e., the Scripture and the Monumenta christiana) and an overemphasis on the
authoritative moments of tradition at the expense of the free-
working of the Spirit in the church.[5] But in Perrone's view,
there is no distinction, for the teaching authority of the
church is not merely her own, but Christ's; she is an organ of
the divinity--the perpetual manisfestation of Christ himself.[6]

This unquestioned identification of divine truth and

[1]Ibid., 18-19.

[2]Kasper, Die Lehre von der Tradition in der Römischen
Schule, pp. 76-78.

[3]Perrone, Praelectiones, IV, 502.

[4]Ibid., 503.

[5]Kasper, Die Lehre von der Tradition in der Römischen
Schule, p. 65.

[6]Perrone, Praelectiones, IV, 236, 241, 243, 256.

historical reality is characteristic of Perrone's concept of
the magisterium, and, Kasper suggests, reflects in a theological context the general mentality of the Restoration
period--that there is a concrete existing order that is at the
same time an expression of the will of God. Perrone shared
the prime concerns of the period for order, unity, and certainty. All three are provided by the authoritative teaching
of the church.[1]

The teaching office in the church has three aspects:
1) that of witness, to propose the truths of faith, 2) that of
judge, to settle controversies that may arise in the understanding of the faith, and 3) that of teacher, in the daily
ministry of instructing the faithful in all things pertaining
to doctrine and morals.[2] Certainty is necessary in all these
aspects and, hence, infallibility pertains to all three.
Since Christ has instituted this office and commanded that all
men should be taught, and God has approved of it by signs and
wonders, it is unthinkable that the church should be able to
err, for then men would be deceived by God. Nor is it think-
able that those who do not accept the teaching of the church
could be condemned if it were not certainly true, nor is there
any reason for those not yet in the church to join it if its
teaching were only probable, for then they would be going merely from one opinion to another.[3]

This infallible, authoritative teaching office has gen-

---

[1]Kasper, Die Lehre von der Tradition in der Römischen
Schule, pp. 56-59.

[2]Perrone, Praelectiones, IV, 139.

[3]Ibid., 140-42.

erally been considered as belonging to the apostles and their
successors as one moral unity, as we mentioned above. Perrone
says that both the ecumenical councils and the dogmatic decrees
of the Roman Pontiff, aequo jure, give solemn and public testimony to the faith which the church professes.[1] The Roman
Pontiff, however, ex divine institutione has supreme authority
over all the bishops of the Catholic Church even assembled in a
general synod. Just as a bishop is superior to a diocesan
synod for no other reason than that he is the bishop, so the
Roman Pontiff is the Episcopus Episcoporum, the Universal
Bishop, and hence, superior to a general council.[2] But this
kind of discussion presumes that there is a possibility that
there could be a separation between head and members (of the
episcopal college) and this is not possible. The Roman Pontiff
only announces what is in the deposit of revelation, and hence,
it cannot be diverse from what the rest of the church professes.[3] Further, the pope does not give a definitive statement until after there has been a long inquisition and thorough
discussion on the local level. This is a matter of historical
fact, he says, and cites the case of Jansenism.[4] If there
should be a division among the bishops, however, there is no
doubt where the error is--"Ubi Petrus, ibi Ecclesia."

Perrone's latter work on the church, L'Idea Cristiana

---

[1]Ibid., 503-04.

[2]Perrone, Praelectiones, IV, 266-67. This along with the
argument that there is no evidence that either the Fathers or
the ancient councils recognized a distinction between the bishops distributive et collective sumptos, which is the only
foundation of the Gallican position, constitutes his answer to
conciliarism.

[3]Ibid., 305-06.

[4]Ibid.

(1862), is a more popular work, somewhat influenced by his
younger colleagues, Passaglia and Schrader, but does not alter
the view outlined here. His increasing devotion to the authority of the Roman Pontiff is reflected in his last work, De
Romani Pontificis infallitilitate, published posthumously in
1874.

The basic ideas of Perrone's ecclesiology and doctrine of
the magisterium, which he shares to some extent with Passaglia
and Schrader and which will be passed on to his successors at
the Gregorian University, can be summed up as follows: The
church is the continuation of the Incarnation--a unity of
divine and human in one (moral) person; the mission and work of
Christ is continued likewise in his church; the human authority
in the church is a necessary condition for faith (never an
object or ground of faith); this authority is not purely human,
but like Christ himself, human-divine. Perrone's favourite
image for all this, as Arévalo shows in his work, is the
"Mystical Body."[1] This theme, along with the generally apologetic and polemical cast of his ecclesiology (the "church"
always means the "Roman Catholic Church" for Perrone) he shares
with his contemporaries, Passaglia and Schrader.

Carlo Passaglia and Clemens Schrader

Although there are significant differences, as far as
their ecclesiology and doctrine of the magisterium are concerned, Passaglia and Schrader may be considered, as Arévalo
says, "one theological personality." We will discuss the biographical details separately, but they were so closely related
theologically that we will treat their teaching as one.

---

[1]For example, Perrone, Praelectiones, IV, 84, 88, 91,
etc.

Of Passaglia, Hocedez says that he was more brilliant and more profound than his teacher and colleague, Perrone, and was to some extent, an innovator.[1] He was certainly a more passionate and controversial man. He entered the Society of Jesus on November 13, 1827, at the age of forty. He did almost all of his studies in Rome, taught physics, mathematics and philosophy at Reggio Emilia and was Prefect of Studies at the German College (1840-44) before returning to the Roman College as Professor of Dogma in 1845. At that time there were two major professors of dogma, Perrone who taught the morning classes, and Passaglia who taught the afternoon session. Precisely how the material was divided at that time we do not know from the Kalendaria. In the academic year 1847-48, he also taught church history. On the 29th of March, 1848, the situation in Rome became precarious because of Mazzini's revolution and all Jesuit communities were dispersed. Passaglia was sent to England to supervise the studies of the Italian scholastics at the temporary scholasticate set up at Lord Hugh Clifford's estate, Ugbrook near Newton, Devonshire. Later that same year, Passaglia accompanied by Schrader and Franzelin, who was at that time still studying and not yet ordained, went to Louvain. He taught dogma there until August 1849, and by December of that year was back in Rome. The following Lent Passaglia preached a series of sermons at the Gesu which were published in the recently founded Civiltà Cattolica and translated into French and German. As a preacher, he was compared throughout Europe to Lacordaire, Newman and Wiseman.

Clemens Schrader was born near Hildesheim in Hanover, studied at the Jesuit gymnasium there and went to the German College in Rome in 1840. He was ordained there in 1846 and two

---

[1]Hocedez, Histoire de la Théologie au XIXe Siècle, II, 355.

years later joined the Society of Jesus and was sent to make
his novitiate with the Italian Jesuits in exile in England. It
was there that he joined Passaglia, accompanied him to Louvain
and also returned to Rome in 1850 as Prefect of Studies at the
German College. The following year he joined the faculty of
the Roman College which had reopened on January 7, 1850. It
was here that the close association between Passaglia and
Schrader began with their joint work, De immaculate Deiparae
semper virginis conceptu (3 vols. Rome: 1854) and their De
ecclesia Christi, the first volume of which was published in
1853.

It is this work that is the best summary of their
ecclesiology and the doctrine of the magisterium. They intended to publish five volumes in this work but only three were
completed. There is no detailed plan of the other two proposed
volumes but Arévalo suggests that "we may be reasonably sure
that books four and five would have concerned themselves with
the properties and notes of the church."[1]

The first three books are very wordy and repetitious but
give an accurate and rather complete picture of their ecclesiology as a whole. The first is a "sort of summary-preview of
the entire treatise" and is a kind of philological approach,
examining the use and meaning of the various words that refer
to the church in the New Testament, the Fathers and early
Christian witnesses, the relation of the church to the syna-
gogue, the various metaphors used in the New Testament to refer
to the church (house, temple, city, kingdom, body), the parables

---

[1]Catalino G. Arévalo, Ecclesiology of Giovanni Perrone,
Carlo Passaglia and Clemens Schrader. Published excerpts from
the unpublished dissertation previously mentioned. (Rome:
Pontificia Universitas Gregoriana, 1959), p. 9.

about the church in the Gospel, the allegories and types of the
church in the early Christian tradition, and, finally, a summary enumerating the various connections between Christ and the
church.[1]

The second book treats of the existence of the church,
its institution by Christ, its continuation in existence, its
perpetuity, visibility, the relation of the infallibility of
the church to its perpetuity, and some scriptual difficulties
against perpetuity.[2]

The third book, which comprises the entire second volume,
treats of the causes of the church--efficient, instrumental,
exemplary, material, formal and final. The discussion of the
magisterium comes under the heading of instrumental cause,
entitled De ecclesiastico ministerio.

The orientation of the entire work, however, even the
third book organized as it is in terms of causes, is much more
scriptual and patristic than philosophical or speculative.
Indeed, at one point in his career, Passaglia was reprimanded
by his superiors for being too "philological and hermeneutic"
and not "scholastic" enough.[3] There are very few citations
from other theologians or from conciliar or papal statements.
The work is a catena of quotations from Scripture and the
Fathers. It has a heavily apologetic and polemical cast. Each
major section of the treatise is followed by argumentation showing that what has been said about the church of Christ is true
of the Roman Catholic church and only of it, not of the

---

[1]Carlo Passaglia, De Ecclesia Christi (Ratisbone, 1853),
pp. 1-80.

[2]Ibid., pp. 81-142.

[3]Arévalo, Ecclesiology of Giovanni Perrone, Carlo
Passaglia and Clemens Schrader, p. 3.

32

Protestant churches.

The dominating result of the analysis of the metaphors, similes and analogies for the church in the New Testament and the Fathers is the unity of Christ and the church. Although they specifically say these are metaphors that they are analyzing and not "proof-texts", they seem to take them rather literally when they draw conclusions about the various connections between Christ and his church. Christ continues per ecclesiam what he began in his physical body, his assumed humanity. He leads men in the way of justice and holiness, frees them from error, gives them the liberty of the sons of God, and brings them to their eternal inheritance. In short, Christ appears visibly among men in ecclesia et per ecclesiam.[1] Passaglia and Schrader even go so far as to say that the communicatio idiomatum exists between the body of the church and Christ the head.[2] This union between Christ and his church is so close that "Christ can no more be separated from the church than from himself," and it is the same union and common existence which applies to the nature and the hypostatsis in Christ, that is, the hypostatic union.[3] Perhaps some greater feeling for the closeness of this union and its consequences may be given by the following citation which is an excellent and accurate summary of their ecclesiology as a whole:

> And so 'Church' does not designate some group of men who follow Christ as their authority and leader; but it is indeed the kingdom of truth, the holy city, the house of faith, the temple of God, the body whose head is Christ, by whose mouth Christ speaks, through which he manifests

---

[1]Passaglia, De Ecclesia, I, 35.

[2]Passaglia, De Ecclesia, I, 35, Communicatio idiomatum is the term used to express the attribution of characteristics proper to one nature in Christ to the person of Christ, thus we can say that God was born of Mary. In this instance, they mean that we can apply characteristics of Christ to the church--thus, they say, Who hears the Church, hears Christ.

[3]Ibid., 80.

himself, and which could not be thought of or understood
for an instant as separated from its head or cut off from
his Spirit.

Consider and reflect now what would necessarily be the
result if the church even once departing from orthodoxy were
to err in doctrine, what Paul would call a Foreign Gospel,
or even a gospel contrary to that which we have announced to
you. It would seem that it would necessarily follow that
the church would no longer be the kingdom of truth, would no
longer be the house of faith, would no longer be the temple
of God, would no longer be the body sustained and directed
by Christ, nor would it any longer be the seat of the Spirit
divinely sent to lead the church to all truth. Indeed, it
would follow from that sentence which Paul continually presents as anathema that the marriage of Christ and the church
would be broken, that Christ would be separated from his own
body, from his own flesh, that he would be divided from himself, that he would be anathema to himself.[1]

It is easy to see how they can say that the church is endowed
with sublime and divine attributes, and that, while the church
may have human imperfections, these are accidental whereas the
divine attributes are intrinsic to her nature.[2] The consequences of this close identification of the church and Christ
for a doctrine of the magisterium will be plain.

Just as the union between Christ and his church is more
than analogous with the union between Christ and His physical
body--it is of the same kind--so the magisterium of the
apostles is of the same kind as the magisterium of Christ.[3] It
has a divine-human character. Just as the Father spoke through
Christ, so Christ speaks through the apostles. The apostles
preached only and all the truth that Christ brought ex sinu
Patris and which the Spirit opened to them. Hence, the
apostolic preaching is divine (since the revelation which is
from God is divine) and has the power and value of a rule
(regula). This divine-human magisterium is the rule of faith
for the Christian. Here Passaglia-Schrader refer to it as the

[1]Ibid., III, 833.

[2]Passaglia, De Ecclesia, II, 127.

[3]Ibid., III, 204.

"objective norm of faith."[1]

This objective norm of faith, the magisterium, has certain qualities following from its divine-human character. It is unified and consistent (since truth itself is unified and consistent, and this is the truth manifested by God to men);[2] it is universal (directed to all nations) and perpetual (till the consumation of the world). This objective norm of faith can neither be added to nor diminished, and is completely immutable because it is divine and perpetual. This objective norm is not subject to any ontological growth or progress nor can it undergo any change the way philosophy and human culture can.[3]

All these qualities are described as "corollaries" or consectaria, things which flow from or can be deduced from the very nature of the normative preaching of the faith by the apostles. In this somewhat vague discussion of the magisterium, Passaglia-Schrader do not make the distinction between the content and the activity of the magisterium which was customary in later treatments of the matter. Schrader, however, in his last work, De theologico testium fonte (written in 1874, but published posthumously in 1878)does not make the distinction between "active" and "passive" tradition but says that they cannot be separated and consequently does not deal with them separately.[4]

This objective norm of faith (the magisterium for Passaglia-Schrader) should be answered by a subjective faith with the same qualities--unified, consistent, universal,

---

[1]Ibid., 212-13.

[2]Ibid., 222.

[3]Passaglia, De Ecclesia, III, 225.

[4]Clemens Schrader, De theologico testium fonte (Paris: Lethielleux, 1878), p. 139.

perpetual, and immutable.[1] They do not deny the development of
faith in the believer nor that there are stages of faith--now
direct, then reflexive, now confused, later distinct. They are
speaking, rather, of the public profession of faith. To achieve
this unity, consistency and universality of faith, the church
must have a faculty, a capability, a suitable means to bring
this about, or, in other words, an infallible teaching authority,
the magisterium.

In arguing that the magisterium is an essential part of
the true Christian church (in somewhat of an apologetic and
polemical context) they say:

> Apostolis adhuc viventibus ecclesiae facies ista fuit, ut
> infallibili magisterio fideles ipsa erudiret, et ad univer-
> salem fidei professionisque unitatem atque concordiam
> revocaret: tum vero rerum naturis accurate unitatem et
> concordiam sine infallibili magisterio obtineri non posse.
> Nullus ergo christianus coetus, qui sibi magisterium
> infallibili non asserat, iure prudenterque vera ecclesia
> existimatur.[2]

The magisterium is necessary, therefore, for unity and truth to
be preserved. There are two major sources (causes) of disunity
possible in the church--error and excessive ambition. But God
has provided against these. Opposed to error is truth, and this
dupliciter, interiorly by faith and exteriorly by the authentic
magisterium of the apostles.[3] Hence, for Passaglia-Schrader,
the authoritative teaching office of the apostles is not a substitute for faith but its external, non-subjective counterpart,
a means of bringing about the unity and universality of faith
when it is threatened by error.

Christ has also provided a means of combating the other

---

[1]Passaglia, De ecclesia, III, 226.

[2]Ibid., 231.

[3]Ibid., 242.

major source of disunity--excessive ambition or avarice
(cupiditas)--interiorly by charity and exteriorly by giving to
the apostles the right of ruling the church in order to obtain
Christian unity.[1] They then cite Mk 10:42-44 as to how the
authority is to be exercised in these activities of the
apostles. There is no doubt, however, that there is authority
in the church. They say that the church, by Christ's author-
ship, is not a democracy but an inequal society in which there
is an order of rulers and an order of subjects.[2]

Joined to these other offices, the apostles were also
designated by Christ as witnesses to the Christian truth.
Christ's promise of the Spirit means that the witness of the
apostles is never just their witness but is always joined to
that of the Spirit. It is more than human; it has a divine-
human character.[3]

Passaglia-Schrader then argue that these four offices of
the apostles--representative (legatus) of Christ, teacher,
ruler, and witness--were intended to be continued and, indeed,
were continued by the apostles and the early church.[4] As evidence for this, they cite 2 Tim 1:5, that the apostles did pass
on these offices, Jn 14:16-17, Mt 28:18-20, Eph 4:15-15, that
Christ intended these to be so continued, and all the terms in
the New Testament that suggest duration, continuity, and perpetuity, e.g., in aeternum, usque ad consummationem saeculi, etc.[5]
The final cause of these offices and their perpetuity explains
why this must be the case: "that through the unity of faith and

---

[1] Ibid., 242-43.

[2] Ibid., 257.

[3] Ibid., 259-60.

[4] Ibid., 273, 297-300.

[5] Ibid., 300.

knowledge of the Son of God we all may come to that full and
absolute maturity of man and pursue that perfection by which the
mystical body of Christ ought to be increased."[1] Further, the
parables about the kingdom--the wheat and cockle must grow
together until the harvest, e.g.--indicate the duration of these
functions until some point in the future.

Passaglia-Schrader then argue that such continuity of
office was actually the case in the early church, offering evidence from all the monumenta Christiana--liturgical texts, canon
and civil law, histories of the individual churches and of the
church as a whole, but especially from the Fathers--Ignatius,
Optatus, Tertullian, Cyprian and Augustine.[2] They summarize the
results of their historical work (and this is basically what
they think they are about)[3] as follows: From the Apostolic age
on there were in the churches ministerial offices with the three
functions of teaching, "pastoring," and witnessing (docendi,
pascendi, and testandi), founded by Christ, directed by the
Holy Spirit, set up or organized by the apostles and propagated
by them, omitting nothing that was conducive to the wise and
legitimate continuation of this ministry.[3]

Besides the historical evidence, Passaglia-Schrader argue
from the purpose of the ministry and the demands of faith to
certain qualities of that ministry. Such a ministry, they say,
had to be protected from error and hence is infallible. Since
obedience to the teaching is necessary for salvation, those who

---

[1]Ibid.

[2]Ibid., 314-25.

[3]"Historical work" for them was the simple citation of
texts from ancient documents which seemed to substantiate the
point they were trying to make. There was no interpretation or
contextual location of the texts nor discussion of the intention
of the ancient author. It was a rather "fundamentalist"
approach to history.

[4]Passaglia, De ecclesia, III, 311.

38

would not believe could not be condemned unless the teaching
were infallible.[1]

Further, not only have such offices continued (this from
historical evidence) but they will and must continue in the
future, in other words, they are perpetual. For the necessity
of protecting the faith, fighting heresy and punishing violators
will continue; hence, these ministries must continue. If they
ceased to be, the church itself would cease to be.[2]

Although they do not argue that this follows directly from
the nature or purpose of the ministry, they cite Irenaeus saying
that those who are presbyters in the church ought to be obeyed,
"because they have by succession of the episcopate, according to
the will of the Father, received the certain charism of truth."[3]
Truth reigns in the church through those who have succeeded the
apostles. The charism is attached to the office.

This three-fold ministry (docendi, pascendi, testandi) is
related to the church in many ways and the church in turn is
closely related to Christ. The ministry (of Christ, of the
apostles, of their successors) precedes the church as a cause
its effects, as a source it's stream.[4] Between the ministry and
the church there is a unity of origin or source. They also
describe the relationship of ministry to church as one of
teachers to pupils, pastors to sheep, witnesses to hearers,
those who enlighten to those to be enlightened, those who perfect to those to be perfected, those who sanctify to those to
be sanctified.[5] Even on the verbal level, it is easy to see how

---

[1]Ibid., 312-13.

[2]Ibid., 320-21.

[3]Ibid., 323.

[4]Ibid., 326.

[5]Ibid., 328.

such a description of functions will become a description of states--those who are enlightened, those who are perfect, etc.

It is important to note that in the De Ecclesia, Passaglia-Schrader always speak of the magisterium as one of the functions of the apostolic college and their successors, never as belonging to the pope or the papacy alone. This is not to say, however, that either Passaglia or Schrader wished to downgrade the primacy. In his earlier treatise, De Praerogativis beati Petri (1850), Passaglia has no doubt that Christ established a primacy of Peter among the other apostles-- "he was designated the foundation of the Church"[1] and had a "primacy of faith" and a principatus in episcopatu fidei.[2] Peter was to support and strengthen his fellow apostles in the faith. Lk 22:32 is cited frequently as the basis for this claim. There is an inequality in the apostolic college itself since Peter is set off from the rest as the "foundation, the bearer of the keys, the one who strengthens (confirmator) and the universal pastor." This is true also of the teaching office. Peter excels, precedes (praecellit) the others.[3] Despite this, however, Passaglia still speaks of the magisterial office as belonging to all the apostles.[4]

In his discussion of the relation of pope and council in the Theses De Conciliis Oecumenicis (1856) the same position on the primacy is presented but the decrees of an ecumenical council are also to be considered free from error and the truest

---

[1]Carlo Passaglia, De Praerogativis beati Petri (Ratisbonae: G. J. Manz, 1850), pp. 201-02.

[2]Ibid., p. 92.

[3]Ibid., pp. 300-01.

[4]Ibid., pp. 159-60.

40

rule of faith.[1] A council, however, cannot be conceived of
without being joined to the pope.[2]

Schrader, in the works written alone which deal with this
subject matter, affirms the primacy more strongly than Passaglia
but still says that Christ conferred the magisterium on the
apostles.[3] The universal magisterium is not for individuals to
exercise, with one exception--the successor to the prince of the
apostles. This is the only case of universal, perpetual magisterium exercised individually.[4] As Schrader grew older he
became more and more ultramontane and in 1862 wrote De Unitate
Romana because of the "contemporary attacks on the dignity and
divine privileges of the Pontiff."[5] The entire book is a
defense of just that. He was one of the strongest supporters of
infallibility on the preparatory commission for Vatican I and,
somewhat symbolically, four years before his death stood on the
walls of Rome ministering to the needs of the papal defenders.[6]

Summary

The founders of the Roman School developed an ecclesiology
based on a renewed study of the Fathers and the early sources of
the Christian tradition which has legitimately been termed a
"Mystical Body" theology. That was the image they favored to

---

[1]Carlo Passaglia, De Conciliis oecumenicis. Edited with
an introduction and notes by Heribert Schauf (Freiburg/Br.:
Herder, 1961), p. 30.

[2]Ibid., p. 16.

[3]Schrader, De theologico testium fonte, pp. 122-23.

[4]Ibid.

[5]Clemens Schrader, De unitate Romana (Freiburg/Br.:
Herder, 1962), p. ix.

[6]Augustus Ferretti, "De vita et scriptis R. P. Clementis
Schrader," in De theologico testium fonte, pp. i-xiv.

express the close relationship between Christ and the church.
With some reliance on Möhler, they conceived of the church as a
continuation of the Incarnation. The church is the Body of
Christ, but not his physical body nor just a moral body. It is
the intimate relationship of body to head that they wish to
stress. Consequently, there is a close identification of Christ
and the church. The two share the same qualities, the same
characteristics, the same attributes. Hence, the teaching
authority, the magisterium, is of a divine-human character. It
is not just the doctrine or men that is taught, but that of the
Spirit. This is a theological explanation of and justification
for the emphasis on authority as the source of unity and order
that was characteristic of the Restoration period in which they
lived. It is from this theological background that Franzelin
works out a more nuanced, systematic and speculative doctrine of
the magisterium.

John Baptist Franzelin

For the theology of the magisterium, Franzelin's work was
not only the ripe fruit of his precedessors but also the fertile
seed of his successors. Even for Burghardt who believes that
the significant development of identifying the magisterium and
tradition did not really come until Billot, the work of
Franzelin was the "framework in which that theology would evolve
in the decades to come."[1] I would even say that there is little
development in the understanding of the magisterium beyond what
is contained, at least implicitly, in Franzelin. It is precisely this dominance by Franzelin that enables us to treat

---

[1]Walter J. Burghardt, "The Catholic Concept of Tradition
in the Light of Modern Theological Thought," *Proceedings of the
Sixth Annual Convention of the Catholic Theological Society of
America*, 1951, Reprint, p. 17.

these theologians as a school.

John Baptist Franzelin was born in Aldein in the Tyrol on
April 15, 1816, had his early schooling at the Franciscan college at Bolzano and entered the Jesuit novitiate at Gratz in
1834. He taught for six years at the colleges of Tarnopol and
Lemberg in Austrian Poland and began his theological studies in
Rome in 1845. He fled Rome in 1848 along with Passaglia and
Schrader and finished his theological studies at Louvain. He
was ordained in 1849 and then taught scripture at the Scholasticate at Vals for a year until he was called to Rome to teach
oriental languages in 1850. He lectured on dogmatic theology in
1851 and became Prefect of Studies at the German college in
1853. In 1857 he returned to the Gregorian University to the
chair of dogmatic theology where he remained until his death on
December 11, 1886. He was a consultor to the Holy Office, was
papal theologian at the First Vatican Council and was named a
cardinal by Pius IX on April 3, 1876.

As a professor of dogmatic theology, Franzelin wrote
"tracts" on most of the theological question,[1] but his most
famous and influential work is the De Divina traditione et
Scriptura (1870). It is this work which contains his thinking
on the magisterium and which we will use as our basic source,
along with the posthumously published De Ecclesia Christi
(1887).

Franzelin assumes that God has spoken to man, but not
immediately to each individual man. Rather, He has revealed
himself to some whom He has then constituted his legates to
promulgate this revelation to others. This self-revelation was

---

[1]For example, Tractatus de SS. eucharistae sacramento et
sacrificio (Rome, 1868), Tractatus de sacramentis in genere
(Rome, 1868), Tractatus de Deo trino secundum personas (Rome,
1870), Tractatus de Verbo incarnato (Rome, 1870).

completed in Jesus Christ and with his apostles but was destined
not only for their contemporaries but for all men ad consummationem saeculi. That this revelation should ever be lost or
deformed is contrary to its character and purpose, i.e., the
salvation of all men. Since this revelation is necessary for
salvation, it must be protected, certainly known (or knowable)
and handed down from the apostles to the entire human race even
down to our own day. The means by which this is done (sive
instrumentis ac monumentis sive organis viventibus ac custodi-
bus) he calls the "principles of Christian knowledge." Here he
is talking about the "objective principles"--those supreme
truths which are the sources of our knowing other truths or
which contain other truths in themselves implicitly. In Christian knowledge, the supreme directing principle and norm is the
known infallible authority of God. This is applied concretely
in our own knowledge through the infallible means by which
revelation comes down to us. The authority of these means
(whether monumenta or the infallible guardians of revelation)
contains the directing principle of all of our knowledge of
revealed truths. But this principle in the abstract is not
something from which the truths of revelation can be derived by
analysis. In the concrete, however, all the revealed truths
can be known from these monumenta (Scripture, the Fathers, etc.)
and from these infallible custodians of the faith. Hence,
these means of preserving and transmitting the revelation contain the "formal directing principle" and the "supreme material
principle" of all Christian knowledge and theology.[1]

"Principle", in other words, means both the norm (formal,

[1]John Baptist Franzelin, De Divina Traditione et Scriptura
(3rd ed.; Rome: S. C. de Propaganda Fide, 1882), "Prologo-
menon," pp. 4-6. (Hereinafter referred to as D.T.).

directing) and the source (material) of Christian knowledge.
This is in contrast, in Franzelin's view, with the Protestant
position of sola scriptura. To him, this means that scripture
is the only source and that there really is no authoritative
norm save the individual himself. The whole discussion takes
place in this polemical context and he is most anxious to refute
the Protestant position (or his understanding of it, at least)
throughout.[1] He feels that the sola scriptura is the most
fundamental Protestant error and destructive of the whole of
ecclesiology.

This is the context, then, in which Franzelin discusses
the magisterium. In the very first thesis of the De Divina
Traditione, he makes the distinction between objective and
active tradition. Tradition in the objective sense is that
which is handed on--doctrines or instruction; in the active
sense it is the acts and means by which the doctrines and practices are handed down to us.[2] Tradition in the active sense
contains the objective sense and the objective sense could not
exist without being preserved and handed on, i.e., the active
aspect. Hence, the two can be distinguished but not separated.
Tradition must always be considered in complexu. But the
integrity, preservation and authority of the content depends on
tradition in the active sense. It is this active sense of tradition, the modus quo, which is the formal, distinguishing element in the complex notion of tradition. Franzelin specifically
uses the analogy of form (active aspect) and matter (objective
aspect) to describe the relationship. It is also this formal
element that distinguishes tradition from Scripture. He cites
the Fathers (Clement of Alexandria specifically) with approval

---

[1]Ibid., pp. 6-8, 46ff., and passim.

[2]Ibid., pp. 11-12.

to the effect that Scripture too is part of the objective
aspect of tradition, traditionem scriptam. The content may be
the same in Scripture and objective tradition; it is the mode
of preservation and propagation that is diverse.[1] The means of
preserving tradition is not by writings, but by "perpetually
self-succeeding guardians of the faith." Hence, we understand
tradition to refer ordinarily to doctrines and practices that
have been handed down from the early church by means other than
the Scripture.

Prior to the question of whether there are such doctrines
and practices that are not found in Scripture or, at least
which cannot be known only from Scripture, is the question of
whether there exists some kind of instrument or means of propagation and conservation other than Scripture by which doctrines
and practices revealed either by Christ himself or by the Spirit
through the apostles could be handed down to us. This question
is prior and more universal since there could never by any certainty about the authority of such tradition unless it can
first be demonstrated that such a means or organ of tradition
has been divinely instituted. Whatever authority such tradition would have is derived from (or rather identified with) the
fact of its divine institution.[2] Further, from Franzelin's
polemical standpoint, this is the basic point of dispute with
the Protestants, for they are forced to deny the existence of
such an organ or means of transmitting the doctrine and practices first revealed by Christ in order to maintain their other
doctrines.[3] Or, more positively, if one admits such a means

---

[1]Franzelin, D.T., pp. 18-19.

[2]Franzelin, D.T., Thesis III, on the method of the tract,
pp. 20-21.

[3]Ibid., pp. 252-53.

46

besides Scripture, then the revealed truths can be known from
these divinely appointed guardians of the deposit, and more particular questions about individual divine traditions ought to be
settled by reference to them. Consequently, for Franzelin, the
first question to be discussed in his treatment of tradition is
the means of preservation and transmission--the authentic magisterium. Having established his own authority as being divine,
Christ commanded complete faith and absolute obedience to his
doctrines, precepts and instructions and that these should be
preached to all men at all times. For this purpose he chose
his disciples and from them selected doctores ac magistros to
whom he communicated the authority and power of teaching,
ruling, and sanctifying and to whom the rest of the faithful
were to be subject. Thus, he constituted his church in which,
as in a rich deposit, he placed all truth.[1] The origin, the
supreme source of the whole subsequent perpetual succession is
God himself-made-man--a personally living magisterium. This
Franzelin calls the primus gradus of Christian doctrine and discipline. The gradus secundus is the authentic magisterium of
the apostles with the charism of the Holy Spirit and with the
whole doctrine to be communicated. He cites the usual loci in
Scripture to show the sending and the conferring of the offices
of docendi et regendi,[2] as well as the promise of the Spirit.[3]

The proper response of the Christian to this conferred
power of teaching and ruling is the obedience of faith. By this
he means the acceptance of the preached word of God, the Gospel,

[1]Ibid., pp. 22-24.

[2]Franzelin, D.T., p. 25--Mt 18:18; Mk 16:15; Lk 14:47 ff;
Jn 20:21; Acts 1:8, 9:15.

[3]Ibid., Jn 14:16, 15:16; 16:23; Lk 14:49; Acts 2; I Pet
1:12; Mt 18:20.

and the expected condemnation of those who refuse it.[1] There is
no attempt at exegesis of these passages of Scripture nor is any
comment made on the possibility of their problematic nature. If
it occurred to Franzelin, he certainly did not indicate that
there was any other possible reading of the texts than the one
he assumes.

From this historical account of the origin of Christian
community, it must be inferred that the authority, the personal
authentic magisterium, the apostolic preaching and the obedience
of faith in response to it, is not something external or accidental to religion or to the Christian economy but rather "an
internal and essential property of the economy instituted by
Christ" and for that reason immutable. Hence, any position that
would exclude the living and authoritative magisterium subverts
the nature of the Christian religion. Franzelin sees the sola
scriptura affirmation of the (as he insists on calling them)
Deformatores as doing just that. The underlying presupposition
of this whole argument is explicitated by Franzelin when he says
that the "preservation is the same as the origin," the "progress
the same as the beginnings."[2] This is said in contrast to the
Protestants (he cites Neander, History of Dogma, I, 76) who con-
tend that there was one economy at the time of the
apostolic origins and another one subsequently, according to
Franzelin. He merely asserts his assumption without any attempt
at validation either historically or otherwise. His essentialist, a-historical viewpoint is most obvious here.

He concludes this thesis with the affirmation that the
"principal instrument for the original promulgation of the

---

[1]Ibid., pp. 26-27--Mk 16:16; I Thess 2:13; Rom 1:5; Cor
10:5, 6.

[2]Franzelin, D.T., p. 28.

48

Christian faith was not only Scripture but the personal authentic magisterium" and that the "living authentic magisterium
remains the organ of perpetual preservation." By the special
providence of God the Scriptures were added as a partial font,
but they were not considered by the apostles as something essential or proper to their apostolate, as is evidenced by the fact
that not all of them wrote nor did they think that all doctrine
had been consigned to writing.

That this living magisterium which Christ conferred on his
apostles was intended by him to be the perpetual organ of the
Christian tradition Franzelin indicates in his next thesis by
citing the words of Jesus promising the Spirit "even to the
consummation of the world."[1] In the promise of the charism of
truth through the Holy Spirit and his own guidance, Christ, as
Franzelin sees it, instituted the perpetual apostolic succession to carry on the office of teaching and witnessing to the
revealed doctrine. That the apostles did pass on this function
to others he argues from the familiar citations in Timothy and
Acts.[2] Not all the charisms of the original apostles were
passed on, however. The fact that they were personally in-
structed by Christ and that they received revelation immediately from him and from the Holy Spirit were gifts that could not
be passed on; otherwise one would have to say that revelation
did not cease with the death of the last apostle, but that new
revelations could continually occur. This he is unwilling to do.
The extraordinary charisms of being apostles (not just bishops) and
of new revelations did not extend beyond the last apostle. But
the words, "teach all nations, baptizing them," and "Behold, I am

[1]Franzelin, D.T., p. 31--Jn 14:16-18, 26, 16:13; Mt 28:20;
Mk 16:15-16; Lk 24:47-49; Acts 1:8.
[2]Ibid., p. 33--2 Tim 1:13-14; I Tim 4:13-16; I Tim 6:13-20;
2 Tim 1:6-8; Acts 20:28-32.

with you until the consummation of the world" announce directly
only the magisterium with its ordinary charism of truth, perennially extended to their successors.[1]

These words, further, were directed to the apostolic college as a whole, to the apostolic body in union with and under
the headship of Peter, so that the universal magisterium and the
charism of infallibility connected with it are not to be understood as having been conferred on the apostles as individuals
(with the exception of the head, Peter). Peter is the exception
because the universal teaching authority and the gift of infallibility connected with it were "ordinary" to Peter. The distinction between ordinary and extraordinary is introduced without much of an explanation and no justification. He says only
that ordinary means that which is perennially passed on to their
successors, and extraordinary is that which is not so transmitted.[2] Why this power should be ordinary to Peter he does not
say. He merely states that it was.

There are two characteristics of the Christian revelation
that make this economy of a perpetually living teaching authority particularly suitable--its universality and its unity. By
this Franzelin means that the revelation must be proposed by a
means adapted to all without the moral possibility of error and
that all the truths of revelation must be expounded. If these
two conditions are not met, then people cannot be obliged to
believe or be condemned for non-belief. The alternatives for
achieving such certainty and completeness about the truths of
revelation are only two, and both are ruled out. God could give
to each individual some supernatural grace or illumination or

[1]Ibid., p. 40.

[2]Franzelin, D.T., p. 40, and J. B. Franzelin, De Ecclesia
Christi (Rome, 1887), p. 115. (Hereinafter referred to as De
Ecclesia.)

immediate revelations, but this has neither been promised, nor
has it existed. If there were no help from God, then man would
have to come to these truths by his own "scientific inquiry,"
but this is impossible both because of the wide diversity of
ability among individuals and because of the nature and difficulty of the truths of faith themselves. Hence, the most
appropriate means of proclaiming the divinely-given revelation
to all men without effort or fear of diminishing it is by
means of authoritative guardians and teachers, divinely sent
and constituted in perpetual self-succession.[1]

Although the suitability argument does not contribute
much to his case that such an authority was in fact divinely
established, it is particularly significant in revealing why he
is so interested in such authority. Not only is it polemically
directed against the Protestant notion of sola scriptura and
what he considers to be the authority of the individual, but
authority is the necessary basis of unity and universality.[2]
Indeed, this authoritative organ is, as it were, the cause of
this unity and universality. We will take this up at greater
length in Chapter IV.

This authoritative teaching body, designed as it was by
Christ to implement these essential characteristics of the
Christian revelation--unity and universality--did not change
either in its function or its authority with the advent of
Scripture or in the life of the church in post-apostolic times.
The New Testament writings did not replace the authentic magis-
terium but presupposed it, and were an instrument in its hands
for the more effacious preservation and explication of the total

---

[1]Franzelin, D.T., pp. 44-47.

[2]Franzelin, De Ecclesia, pp. 148, 254, 386.

deposit.[1] Franzelin then offers a catena of citations from the
Fathers of the first, second and third centuries to show that
the early church understood this continuing apostolic succession
as the visible organ for preserving and propagating the complete
doctrine of Christ. His argumentation here is that the changes
in the historical situation of the church--even the advent of
Scripture and the expansion and challenges of the first three
centuries--the "accidentals" as he calls them--did not affect
the economy instituted by Christ because that is an "essential"
of the church. As something essential, it is necessarily
immutable.

Up to this point we have been presenting Franzelin's
answer to his question as to whether there exists a means of
propagation and conservation of the divine revelation other than
Scripture. Upon examining the words of Christ, the actions of
the apostles and the words and deeds of the early church, he
concludes that there is a visible organ for the preservation and
propagation of the deposit of faith, an authentic magisterium.
It was instituted by Christ and was intended by him to perdure to
the end of time fulfilling the same function of preserving and
propagating the divine revelation, in other words, it is
perpetual and immutable.

Now we are in a position to ask more specifically just
what this organ is, how it functions, who exercises it, and how
it relates to the rest of the Christian community. For
Franzelin, the authentic magisterium is the "successors of the
apostles united in perpetual succession and in mutual communion
through the charism of truth guarding the deposit of faith."[2]

---

[1]Franzelin, D.T., pp. 56-64.

[2]Ibid., p. 64.

In his summary thesis on tradition when he draws together all
the elements he has previously discussed, the organ for transmitting the doctrine of the faith is described as "the guardians
of the deposit and divinely instituted teachers in continuous
succession and unanimously with the assistance of the Holy
Spirit."[1] The magisterium then, is the same thing as traditio
activa. Whether or not it is absolutely accurate to say that
Franzelin identifies the magisterium and tradition is a matter
of some dispute in the literature. It seems to come down to a
discussion about a quatenus rather than to be a substantive disagreement. The literature is clearly and adequately surveyed by
Mackey, and I agree with his conclusion: "It is quite true that
Franzelin does not say in so many words that Tradition is identical with magisterium, but without using that precise expres-
sioniit is hard to see how he could have more definitely proposed the same idea."[2] It is this continuing authoritative
teaching body that makes tradition to be what it is, i.e., its
ratio formalis.

The source of the authority in this authoritative teaching
body, the magisterium, is the "charism of truth," "the charism
of infallibility," "the assistance of the Holy Spirit"--they are
all the same for Franzelin.[3] The Holy Spirit is the adequate
and efficient cause of the preservation of the revelation. This
is in the form of "assistance," "direction," or "protection,"

---

[1]Ibid., p. 96.

[2]J. P. Mackey, The Modern Theology of Tradition (New York:
Herder & Herder, 1963), p. 12.

[3]Franzelin, D.T., p. 96. "insuper demonstratum est,
verbis disertis instituisse Christum, ut magisterium authenti-
cum, cuius auctoritas est ex assistentia Spiritus Sancti
inductentis in omnem veritatem, primo ordinatum ad infallibilem
promulgationem revelationis sit perpetuum usque ad consummationem saeculi ad eiusdem integrae revelationis conservationem
et propagationem."

not in the form of new or continuous revelations. The apostles
alone were constituted by Christ as "organs of new revelations"
but not their successors. The "assistance" that is given to
their successors does not exclude nor can it operate without the
human elements--investigation, care, ingenuity--all of which are
under the action and direction of the Holy Spirit as "a visible
body informed by an invisible spirtual charism."[1]

To whom is this charism given, then? The charism given to
the apostles refers immediately to them and their successors as
its subject, but to the whole church for its use and growth.[2]
Or, more definitely, he says that infallibility in teaching is
given to all those and only those who have the ius et officium
divinitus commissum authentice docendi universam Ecclesiam, or
again, to the "body of pastors and teachers in union with and in
consensus with and subordination to the visible head of the
church."[3] The "infallibility in teaching" is distinguished from
the gift of "infallibility in believing" which is given to the
entire church. The two can be distinguished but not separated
since the profession of the faith of the believing church is the
end and purpose toward which the office of preaching and teaching is ordered.[4] Franzelin refers to the charism given to pastors and teachers as a gratia externa, meaning, it seems, a
charism that has some external or visible manifestation as con-
trasted with the invisible or internal action of the Holy Spirit
in other ways in the church.[5]

Franzelin stresses the view that the "promises" were not

[1]Ibid., pp. 36 ff, 80-82, 165, and Franzelin, De Ecclesia,
p. 325.

[2]Franzelin, D.T., p. 106.

[3]Ibid., p. 115.

[4]Ibid., p. 104.

[5]Ibid., p. 106.

given to the successors of the apostles as individuals because
individuals did not succeed the apostles in the office of
authentically teaching the universal church (that was a personal
charism of the apostles alone), but the promises were to the
successors of the apostles as a corporate body, in communi,
quatenus sunt Ecclesia docens.[1] This should not be read, however, as an affirmation of collegiality in the sense in which
one might understand that after Vatican II. If anything, on the
contrary, it is a down-grading of the rights and responsibility
of the individual bishops vis-à-vis the universal church.

The one exception to this corporate functioning of the
ecclesia docens is Peter and his successors who may exercise the
charism individually, for Peter received this office and function as ordinary, not extraordinary (cf. supra.) For this
position, Franzelin cites Mt 16:18, Jn 21:22 and Lk 22:32--
"strengthen your brothers." Further, the ecclesia docens does
not exist except insofar as it is in union with and subordinate
to the visible head of the church, the Roman Pontiff. Indeed,
although the causa efficiens of the infallibility of the
ecclesia docens is the promise of the assistance of the Spirit
of Truth, the conditio sine qua non and the causa formalis is
the visible head of the church and the union and consensus of
the members with this head.[2]

This does not suggest in Franzelin's mind that there are
two adequately distinct subjects of the charism of infallibility. Rather, in his words, "it is both the visible head of the
church per se spectatum, and this visible head insofar as it is
so constituted (as head and body) that is infallible with the

---

[1] Ibid., p. 115

[2] Ibid., p. 115; Franzelin De Ecclesia, p. 124.

assistance of the Spirit of truth."[1] Thus they are inadequately
distinct in accordance with the definition of Vatican I, which
he cites at this point (Constitution I, de Ecclesia Christi,
Chapter IV). If not completely distinct, however, there is no
doubt in Franzelin's mind that the cathedra apostolica, the
Roman Pontiff, is the supreme authentic magisterium whose
definitive doctrinal pronouncement obliges the universal church.
The bishops are united with the pontiff but subordinate to him.[2]
The authority for the doctrinal care of the universal church
resides per se et primo in the one pastor of the whole church
and in no other single person. This extraordinary position of
Peter and his successors is clear to Franzelin merely from the
classical scriptural loci. There is no need in his mind for
detailed exegesis. Further, his emphasis on the papal prerogatives is still in opposition to the Gallican or Febronian position which he seems to find lurking behind every mention of
episcopal consensus.[3]

The magisterium for Franzelin, then, is confined to those
who have the office in succession to the apostles. This would
seem to exclude the Fathers and theologians, except insofar as
they happen to coincide with such an office. He does hedge a
bit, however. The Fathers taken individually are not infallible, but we should not regard their theological opinions
lightly. A consensus of the Fathers on a doctrine of faith
could not be contrary to the faith and thus corrupt tradition.
This is not because of their individual infallibility or the
intrinsic merit of their opinions but rather because of the

---

[1]Franzelin, D.T., p. 117.

[2]Franzelin, D.T., pp. 118, 148; Franzelin, De Ecclesia,
pp. 254, 386.

[3]Ibid.

56

promise of Christ.[1] If there is an opposition between the consensus of the Fathers of one age and the consensus of the
Fathers of another period, it cannot be a true opposition in re
ipsa, but must be presumed to be apparent only, and in the "manner of speech." If such a lack of contradiction cannot be shown
from purely historical or hermeneutical principles, it can
nevertheless be demonstrated from a theological principle,
namely that because of the promise of Christ to the church the
Spirit speaks through the Fathers.[2] This, however, is not the
charism of infallibility or of assistance to the magisterium.
The Fathers basically have two functions--witness to the tradition and teachers (private).

Theologians too are witnesses to the tradition and pre-
eminently the "learning Church." Their teaching cån avoid error
by the "obedience of faith" to those to whom the charism of
truth was promised.[3] But the constant and unanimous opinion of
theologians can certainly establish what the "catholic understanding" of the magisterium is and was, and their work is a
preparatory element out of which magisterial statements are
made. It would be "temerarious" to ignore their opinions.[4]
The Fathers and theologians, then, are witnesses and teachers
but do not share the charism which is the source of authority
and authenticity. They are not the magisterium.

Beside the characteristic of apostolic succession, there
is another criterion that is very important in Franzelin's mind
for locating and delimiting the charism of truth (which is the

[1]Franzelin, D.T., p. 173.
[2]Ibid., 180-81.
[3]Ibid., p. 205.
[4]Ibid., p. 209.

basis of this authority), and that is the consensus of the apostolic succession. By this he means union and communion among the successors of the apostles and especially with the center of unity, the Bishop of Rome. The charism is not present when this consensus is not present, and, more affirmatively, an authoritative tradition can be said to exist when such a consensus can be demonstrated.[1] A consensus with the present alone is not sufficient; it must also be a consensus with the past. The consensus can, however, be just as much an effect of a magisterial statement as its cause.[2] He even goes so far as to say that a pronouncement by the pope alone can bring about such a consensus. (That was in 1870!)

Consensus on a broader scale, among the faithful or the church as a whole, also plays a part in Franzelin's thought, but not an "active" part. The "sense of the faithful" is significant only insofar as it is in relationship to the authentic magisterium, and the relationship is one of subordination, of obedience. The faith is preserved in its integrity in the community of the faithful, not by the immediate operation of the Holy Spirit or without a visible ministry, but through the authentic magisterium of the apostolic succession. The infallibility which the faithful enjoy is described as "passive."[3] It is an infallibility in credendo, or in fidei obedientia as as opposed to an infallibility in docendo or in fidei praedicatione ac definitione. This consensus among the church as a whole is, however, one means by which the pope can come to the knowledge of a doctrine as definable--but only one of

---

[1] Ibid., p. 118.

[2] Ibid., p. 111.

[3] Ibid., pp. 120-21.

several possible means.[1] Again Franzelin is very wary of anything that smacks of Gallicanism, and in the discussions during
the drafting of the constitution _Pastor aeternus_ the view had
been put forth that the pope was obliged to determine if a consensus of the whole church existed before he could exercise the
magisterial power. This view Franzelin opposed. He does point
out, however, that as a matter of fact Pius IX had consulted
the other bishops to discover what the attitude of their faithful was before defining the dogma of the immaculate conception.[2]
He wishes to indicate by this that the consensus of the faithful
is to be considered among the criteria of divine tradition, but
not a means of its authoritative passing on.

Perhaps somewhat more briefly we can answer the question
as to what is the object of this authoritative teaching power.
Or, what kinds of things can be taught? Franzelin says that
the "deposit of the Christian faith, taken in a strict sense,
embraces all and only those things revealed by God explicitly
or implicitly to the human race to be believed, performed or
followed; or, in other words, those things made known in the
universal (_catholica_--distinguishing from private revelations)
revelation for the eternal salvation of the human race.[3] He
understands this to include "theoretical doctrinal truths concerning mysteries and dogmas," practical laws, including the
natural law written in the hearts of men, the fundamental
structures of the church, its power and form of government,
things pertaining to sacred worship--sacraments and sacrifice,
in short, the supernatural dogmatic, ethical, juridical and

---

[1] _Ibid._, p. 118.

[2] _Ibid._, p. 111.

[3] _Ibid._, pp. 120-21.

liturgical orders. These truths may be in the deposit implicitly and only gradually explicitated and proposed. What is
preserved in the deposit is not only the words and formulas but
the "understanding" (sincerae intelligentiae) of the revealed
truths. This includes the understanding (catholicus intellectus)
of the truths contained in Scripture, for Scripture is authentically interpreted by the magisterium which has the assistance of
the Holy Spirit.[1] The verbal formulas, however, as well as the
meanings must be believed with an "irreformable and immobile"
faith, for there is nothing in the definitions or dogmas "which
is not objectively revealed and immutably true."[2] Other categories may have to be used to deal with other problems at a
later time, but the concepts developed to respond to a particular problem at a particular time (e.g., in the Christological
or Trinitarian controversies) remain true for all time.

This "material object" of the magisterium for Franzelin is
obviously rather all-inclusive. All that the Christian needs to
know certainly for his eternal salvation can be found in this
living magisterium. Hence, this is the "proximate rule of
faith." Although the Word of God is the regula ac norma of
belief for the universal church, it is a rule which must be
explained and is in actu primo only. It is explained and proposed by the living magisterium and then is the regula fidei in
actu secundo. For the truth that is revealed in the Word of God
is not revealed immediately to each individual but is "truth in
custody," the custody of the visible magisterium.[3]

Although I have made passing references to Franzelin's

---

[1] Ibid., p. 216.

[2] Ibid., pp. 305-06.

[3] Ibid., pp. 167-68; Franzelin, De Ecclesia, pp. 382-83.

De Ecclesia, most of the exposition of his thought has been
based on the De Divina Traditione et Scriptura. There is no
difference in the two works on the doctrine of the magisterium.
The De Ecclesia is perhaps a bit more juridical in emphasis and
organization--his concern with the distinction and interrela-
tionship of the potestas magisterii and potestas jurisdictionis, for example--and there is greater preoccupation with
the position of the Roman Pontiff and the monarchical organization of the church.[1] And despite the fact that he uses the
images of the Bridegroom and the Bride and the Corpus Christi
mysticum to describe the relationship of Christ to his church,
the dominant image for the church is that of Kingdom--the
regnum veritatis et sanctitatis.[2] Christ himself gave his
church the form of a monarchy, and this cannot be changed.[3]
Regnum, regimen, potestas, are the categories most often
employed to describe or define the church. There is little or
no consideration of the eschatological nature of this kingdom.

What is perhaps most amazing of all is that there is
little or no mention of the function of councils (ecumenical
or local) as part of the magisterium at all. Various conclusions are possible but the fact that a man who was the papal
theologian at a council in session the same year that his major
work was published does not discuss the councils as magisterial
is astounding. He certainly cites conciliar statements as
magisterial and authoritative teaching and considers the
bishops in communione as the magisterium, but there is no explicit discussion of a council as the magisterium. There is no

---

[1]Cf. for example, the statement of Thesis X, De Ecclesia,
pp. 382-83.

[2]Ibid., pp. 47, 65, 77, 79, 89-90.

[3]Ibid., pp. 124 ff.

doubt that he considers the bishops in council as exercising the
magisterial power, but the relationship of this form of the
magisterium to the papal magisterium is treated only so far as
to affirm their union with and subordination to the Roman Pontiff. Conciliar theology seems to have held no interest for
him.

Perhaps we can now summarize Franzelin's notion of the
magisterium in his own words taken from his last work:

> Christ himself, the unus magister, having completed the
> revelation of the faith through himself and through the
> sending of the Holy Spirit to the apostles and by divine
> instructions for the purpose of guarding and explaining
> the whole deposit, remains perennially in his church
> through his delegates who organized themselves in per-
> petual succession and who are protected always by the
> charism of truth and his own presence and who teach in
> his name and with his authority.[1]

All the elements of the notion of the magisterium of the
Roman School are contained in the above, and we will see them
recurring in Franzelin's successors: the close identification
of the magisterium with Christ and the consequent elevation of
its authority to the more-than-human level, the assumption that
all truth necessary for salvation is already contained in the
"deposit," that there is some semi-magical device, the "charism
of truth," given by God to the apostles and their successors in
office, that the main function is to protect something already
possessed. Further analysis of the implications of these
characteristics will be taken up after we have examined their
expression and elaboration in the other professors at the
Gregorian University.

---

[1]Franzelin, De Ecclesia, p. 32.

CHAPTER III

THE THEOLOGY OF THE MAGISTERIUM AT THE

GREGORIAN UNIVERSITY--LATER REPRESENTATIVES

Palmieri and Mazzella

Between the two luminaries of our period--Franzelin and

Billot--there were two theologians at the Gregorian University

who dealt with the notion of the magisterium, Domenico Palmieri

and Camillo Cardinal Mazzella. We will deal primarily with Pal-

mieri, since, after reading through both of them, it is clear

that Mazzella adds little if anything to what Palmieri says on

this topic, and to treat them both at length would be repetitious.

Hence, we will refer to Mazzella only in passing.

Palmieri was born at Piacenza on July 4, 1829, was ordained

and entered the Society of Jesus at the age of twenty-three. He

taught philosophy, theology and Scripture at the seminary of

Fermo and the college of Spoleto until he became professor of

philosophy at the Gregorian University in 1861. From 1867 until

1878, he was professor of dogma there, and for the last five

years of that period he also taught Scripture. From 1878 until

1894, he taught exegesis at Maastricht and then returned to Rome

as theologian to the Sacred Penitentiary and consultor to the

Holy Office. He was also on the Commission for the Code of

Canon Law. He wrote tracts on almost all the usual areas[1] and

shared both the concern for positive theology of Franzelin and

---

[1]For example, Tractatio de Deo creatore (Rome, 1868-69),
De gratia divina (Rome, 1869-70), Tractatus de Deo creante et
elevante (Rome, 1878), Tractatus de poenitentia (Rome, 1879),
Tractatus de gratia divina actuali (Galopiae, 1885), Tractatus
de matrimonio christiano (Rome, 1880), Tractatus de peccato
originali et de immaculatu beatae virginis deiparae conceptu
(Rome, 1904), Tractatus theologicus de novissimis (Prati, 1908),
Tractatus de ordine supernaturali et de lapsu angelorum (Prati,
1910), as well as some commentaries on Scripture and a seven
volume work on moral theology.

63

64

the philosophical competence of Billot. He excelled both,
however, in independence and originality of thought--a virtue
which led him into some temporary disfavor in Rome. As a pupil
of Tongiorgi, he tended to a more dynamic philosophy and
believed that hylomorphism was incompatible with contemporary
scientific knowledge. He rejected the traditional scholastic
theory of the species impressa and offered an explanation of the
persistence of the appearances in the eucharist that was somewhat diverse from the commonly accepted one. In the face of the
Thomistic revival, he was a maverick.

Mazzella was much more a part of the philosophical and
theological "establishment" and, subsequently, became a cardinal.
Born in 1833 at Vitulan, he entered the Jesuits in 1857 and,
after studying and lecturing at Lyons, he helped to found and
taught at the Jesuit theologate at Woodstock, Maryland, from
1867 until 1878 where his major work dealing with the subject of
the magisterium, the treatise De religione et ecclesia, was
first published in 1877.[1] He was requested by Leo XIII to take
the chair of dogmatic theology at the Gregorian in 1878, which
he held for only seven years. He is more apologetically oriented
than Palmieri and not as fully developed on the doctrine of the
magisterium. Further, Palmieri is a better index of whatever
development from Franzelin took place during this period.

It is interesting and indicative that Palmieri's treatment of the magisterium occurs in his work entitled De Romano
Pontifice. Although the work was first published in 1877, the
second edition, which I will follow, contains an addition to the

---

[1]This went through five editions. He also published other
tracts such as De Deo creatore (Woodstock, 1872-73), De
virtutibus infusis (Woodstock, 1875), De gratia Christi
(Woodstock, 1878), De Deo creante (Woodstock, 1877).

Prolegomenon, de Ecclesia, on the magisterium.[1] This addition, however, is eighty-seven pages in length in comparison with the section de infallibili magisterio Romani Pontificis which is one-hundred and seventy-two pages in length. It is not insignificant either that the section de ecclesia is a Prolegomenon. This fact in itself should not be made to support too heavy a conclusion, but there is much evidence to indicate a shift from the notion in Perrone, Passaglia, Schrader and Franzelin that the magisterium is a charism given to the apostolic college and its successors as a body, to a notion in Palmieri of the magisterium as an exercise of an authority or power located immediately and directly in the Roman pontiff and only derivatively in the rest of the bishops associated with him. This will become obvious, as we proceed.

From the beginning of his discussion of the church there is a noticeable shift in emphasis away from the organic conception that had originated with Möhler and been filtered down through Perrone, Passaglia and Schrader to Franzelin and whose underlying theory of incarnatio continuata stressed the close relationship between Christ and the church, and whose characteristic scriptural image was the "Mystical Body." Palmieri gives only a nod in that direction[2] and proceeds to define the church as "the kingdom of Christ on earth ruled by the apostolic authority."[3] In discussing the institution of the church by Christ, the emphasis is on the ministry--in instituting the ministry, Christ instituted the church--and on the power and

---

[1]Domenico Palmieri, De Romano Pontifice (2nd ed.; Prati: Giachetti, Filii et Soc., 1891). There was a third edition in 1902 and a fourth edited by Joseph Filograssi, S.J., in Rome in 1931, indicating something of its continuing use at the Gregorian University and its influence. (Hereinafter referred to simply as Palmieri.)

[2]Brief mention of the images of Corpus Christi and Sponsa Christi on pp. 2, 13, 40-41.

[3]Palmieri, p. 25.

authority in the ministry. All the qualities or functions that
constitute a religious body are achieved through the "triple
power" (of teaching, ruling and sanctifying) and the subordination due to that power.[1] More specifically in the church of
Christ the purpose is the sanctity and eternal salvation of all
men. This is obtained through the exercise of the triple power
given to the apostles and their successors and by the subordination due it--"the authority of the pastors" and the "subjection of the flock."[2]

The church has both an external visible form and an
internal invisible principle in which the supernatural life of
the members consists and which proceeds from Christ. These two
can be compared to "body" and "soul." The interior gifts of
faith, hope, and charity, however, come to individuals through
their association and unity with the church and hence, through
the ministry. This external formal principle--the authoritative
ministry--is a necessary means for the interior principle also.
This authority can "not undeservedly be called the soul of the
church."[3]

This authority and power in the church is not merely human
authority. By divine institution the church is divided into
clerics and laity and the clerics have the authority. This
authority is not founded on reason on which natural societies
are organized but on the divine will. Power and authority in
the church is "supernatural."[4] Likewise, who has this power is
not a matter of reason or of community decision. For the power
is not given immediately and directly to the community as a whole,
but to the pastors directly. Theirs is not a derived authority

---

[1]Ibid., p. 3. [2]Ibid., p. 12. [3]Palmieri, p. 46.

[4]Ibid., pp. 59-61, 116, 205, 235, 287; Camillus Mazzella,
De Religione et Ecclesia (5th ed.; Rome: Forzani et Socii, 1896),
pp. 414-16. (Hereinafter referred to as Mazzella.)

but one immediately from God. This visible authority is manifested in and focused in the magisterium.[1]

Palmieri begins his discussion of the magisterium in
general (as opposed to the papal magisterium) by repeating
Franzelin's point that the ecclesiastical magisterium is the
basic issue between Protestants and Roman Catholics. In contrast
to the Protestant principle of sola scriptura, Palmieri asserts
what he calls the Catholic antithesis: that Christ wished the
doctrine of the faith to be handed on not only in writing but
verbally also, and consequently He instituted both methods for
his church. Christ instituted a personal, living magisterium
endowed with the authority of teaching in his name and the
corresponding obligation on others of hearing and believing
whatever it teaches. This magisterium Christ wished to be perpetual. He has subjected all his flock to it, and it acts in
his place until he comes. He committed to it all power of ruling
and sanctifying.[2] Palmieri then proceeds with a textual exegesis
of the usual passages (Mt 28:18; Mk 16:15) to show that Christ
instituted it in the apostles and that there are two formalities
that can be distinguished but not separated in it--that of witness and that of teacher. This apostolic magisterium, however,
does not operate on its own without any norm. The Word of God,
whether written or revealed to them by the Spirit is the norm to
which they are bound. Christ also ordained that they should
not deviate from this norm--by divine will there is an intimate
connection between the written Word of God and the Word of God
revealed to the apostles.[3] Hence, the apostolic magisterium
both knows the divine relelation certainly, and cannot deviate
from that revelation in proposing it and handing it on to others,

[1]Palmieri, pp. 162-63.

[2]Palmieri, pp. 163 ff; Mazzella, pp. 606-12.

[3]Palmieri, pp. 171-72.

68

i.e., the magisterium is infallible. Palmieri gives the same
arguments as Franzelin as to why this has to be so (cf. p. 53).

This apostolic testimony is the certain and infallible
norm of faith for men. In other words, the magisterium is the
regula fidei.[1] It is carefully distinguished from the motive
of faith, however. The motive is the authority of God revealing
himself. This magisterium is the supreme judge in all questions
of faith and the authentic and necessary interpreter of Scripture.
It was intended by Christ to be perpetual. Palmieri's basis for
this is the usual scriptural citations and the more explicit
argument that the church should always exist as Christ instituted
it, that no human power can change the constitution of Christ's
kingdom, and that he instituted it as a society of masters and
disciples. The very foundation of the church is authority--the
authority of governing and teaching.[2] Thus, the authority of a
personal magisterium is and ought to be perpetual in the church.
This can only be by continual succession (a statement he seems
to take as obvious since he offers no proof nor consideration
of alternative possibilities). The successors of the apostles
as the magisterium were those called bishops in the New Testament.
It is interesting to note that at this point he stresses the
fact that instructions and promises of Christ to teach and
baptise all nations were given to a group, an ordo, the apostolic
college, not to one person. The successors must be an ordo also,
a collegium and there was no other such body in the New Testament
or in the early ecclesiastical documents except the bishops.[3]

The purpose of the magisterium is to guard and protect
the revelation that was complete with the apostolic age, not to
provide new and subsequent revelations. These guardians
(custodes) teach only what Christ taught the apostles. This he

---

[1]Palmieri, pp. 174-205. [2]Ibid., p. 179. [3]Ibid., p. 183.

calls "public tradition."[1] This is not to say, however, that
there could be no progress or growth in the explications or
clarification of known revelation. He reconciles "scientific
progress" and the "immobility of apostolic doctrine" by seeing
it as progress from a less clear and confused notion to a clear
and distinct idea of the doctrine.[2] The Cartesian approach to
truth shows itself most clearly here.

What is contained in the deposit of revelation that the
magisterium is to guard and protect? What is the proper object
of this teaching authority? It is all revealed truths, as well
as those so closely connected as to be necessary for the defense
of revealed truths (dogmatic texts, dogmatic facts, e.g.). In
other words, all those truths whose knowledge is necessary or
useful for preserving the integrity of dogma or the salvation of
souls.[3] This includes anything that might threaten the integrity
or violate the purity of the faith. There are many errors, he
says, which, although not directly opposed to revealed truths,
might deflect the faithful from the path of salvation. Further,
the magisterium's infallibility extends even to the verbal
formulas. Doctrine is proposed per signa sensibilia; and the
church must be able to say what it wants to say, otherwise
infallibility would be useless, and the church would not be able
to fulfill her function of leading men to salvation.[4]

The magisterium is also, as we have mentioned, the authentic and necessary interpreter of Scripture. Even if Scripture
were clear in all places, which it is not, especially when we
consider that it is addressed to all the faithful, it would still
be necessary to have an authentic interpreter, for whatever
knowledge man could obtain by himself would still be human

---

[1]Palmieri, p. 184, 188, 190.   [2]Ibid., pp. 190-94.

[3]Ibid., pp. 223, 225; Mazzella, pp. 622 ff.

[4]Palmieri, p. 228.

knowledge and per se fallible. What the magisterium adds in
interpreting Scripture is certitude of a higher order--a divine
infallible certitude.[1] As far as authority goes, Scripture and
the magisterium are equal, but as related to us, the magisterium
has priority. Scripture is an instrument, and the magisterium
is the authentic interpreter. It is the magisterium, and not
the Scripture, that is necessary for the propagation of the
Gospel and the foundation of the Church.

Although we will treat this more at length in the next
chapter, it is worth noting here that the concern for certitude
is a dominant one for Palmieri. Any anxiety and possible
suspicion about divine matters cannot be tolerated.[2]

One other thesis that indicates a slight drift toward a
more juridicial notion of the magisterium is the assertion that
the teaching authority in the church which imposes an obligation
of believing on the faithful is part of, a species of, the power
of jurisdiction.[3] In Franzelin an act of jurisdiction might on
occasion accompany an act of the magisterium but the teaching
authority was not considered a part of the power of jurisdiction.
It is the power if imposing an obligation that interests
Palmieri. This, he says, is part of the power of binding and
loosing which is the power of jurisdiction. He would subsume
the power of teaching authoritatively under this.

Two characteristics of the truths of Christian doctrine
for Palmieri are worth mentioning here. They are antiquity and
universality. In contrast to human knowledge, which is incomplete
at the beginning, uncertain and mixed with error, truth in the
church of Christ cannot be something new, but is that which was
handed down from the apostles and the earliest members of the

---

[1]Ibid., p. 236.   [2]Ibid.

[3]Ibid., p. 240; Mazzella, pp. 583-88.

church. That which the apostles have not handed down cannot be divine truth, the object of divine faith. Illud ergo verum, quod prius.[1] Universality can be taken both positive and exclusive. That which has been held universally must be ancient and therefore from the apostles. Universality in this case is one sign of antiquity and seems to be reduced to it. If some doctrine has not been held universally, that is not a sure sign that it is not from the apostles, but it at least bears further inquiry. It may, however, be reason for excluding it from the things to be believed. Universality does not have to be proven by interrogating all possible individuals, but frequently only one! For example, Augustine on the question of the gratuity of grace, having been approved by the Holy See, is sufficient to indicate universality. This is hardly universality in any historical or scientific sense, but perhaps in what Franzelin referred to as a "theological sense." Palmieri says that a consensus of the Fathers of the Western church suffices, for "that part of the world suffices in which the Lord wished the first apostles to be crowned with martyrdom."[2] Further, one does not have to show even that the first and second centuries believed something for us to be able to say it is of apostolic origin. It is sufficient to show that some subsequent age held it, since in each age the magisterium is infallible.

The question about the magisterium that is of prime importance for Palmieri, in contrast to Franzelin and his predecessors is the question of who exercises it. The concern with the position of the Roman Pontiff that followed the First Vatican Council is reflected in the book itself. The de Ecclesia is a Prolegomenon and occupies 293 pages whereas the treatise De Romano Pontifice gets 473 pages and is the basis of the entire

[1]Palmieri, p. 246. [2]Ibid., p. 247.

work. The two tracts cannot be separated, he says, and indeed
are closely related in his mind. The De Romano Pontifice is
also titled De Ecclesiae capitate, and in his introduction to it
he says that it is really a question of knowing more accurately
the subject of the power of jurisdiction in the church, i.e.,
Who exercises it. Since he also considers the teaching authority
a subsidiary of the power of jurisdiction, it is a question of
who exercises the teaching authority in the church. The question
is of the subject of the universal magisterium--is it only an
ecomenical council, or only the pope, or both? He formulates
it in another and somewhat revealing way: Whom do we know for
sure from divine revelation was promised the gift of infallibility?[1]

The first part of the tract is concerned with the primacy—
its institution and succession. His main theses are taken from
the Dogmatic Constitution, Pastor aeternus, of Vatican I,
Session IV, which it is not necessary to repeat here.[2] The
second section is concerned with the power of the Roman Pontiff,
both within the church and in relation to societies distinct
from the church itself. It is under this general heading that
he speaks of the infallible magisterium of the Roman Pontiff.
The entire discussion is framed in juridical terms--concerned
with power, jurisdiction, validity.[3] He is most concerned with
refuting the Gallican position.[4] There is no question that the
pope and a council together are infallible; the only problem is
whether either or both can exercise the infallible teaching
authority by themselves. His answer is, of course, that the

[1]Palmieri, p. 594.

[2]Ibid., pp. 296-391; D.S., 3050-3075; T.C.T., 201-220.

[3]To cite just one page, for example, p. 515, where potestas
appears ten times, jurisdictio three times, and regimen three
times.
[4]Palmieri, pp. 596, 599, 633, 640, et passim.

pope is infallible ex sese, without the necessity of consultation with or confirmation by a council, whereas a council cannot
exercise the infallible teaching authority independently of the
pope. His argument is based on the importance of authority.
Authority is what is most necessary in a society; it is the
principle of stability and unity in a society; the whole society
depends on it, and it is necessary for all who wish to be in
that society to adhere to that authority by which the society is
ruled.[1] There must be a subject of supreme authority in the
church. But it cannot be the council as a whole, for then one
would be in the Gallican position of saying that the pope was
subordinate to a council, when, as a matter of fact, a council
cannot act infallibly without the confirmation of the pope.
Hence, the supreme authority is not in a council as a whole and
of itself. But supreme authority must reside in some subject.
Hence, it can only be in the pope.[2]

He says much the same thing in another way when he argues
that (in answer to his formulation of the question) Peter is
the one to whom the gift of infallibility and jurisdiction was
clearly promised in Scripture,[3] and therefore the firmitas of
the faith of the church rests, depends, on the solidity of the
faith of Peter, but the faith of Peter is firm or indefectible
(he later equates firmitas with infallibilitas)[4] ex sese or
infallible ex sese.[5] Supreme authority can only reside in one
who is dependent on no others and on whom all others depend.

Besides such "rational" argument, he has theses showing
that the form of government in the church is a monarchy jure
divino and that all jurisdictional power is immediately in the

[1]Palmieri, p. 311. [2]Ibid., p. 626. [3]Ibid., pp. 351 ff.
[4]Ibid., p. 605. [5]Ibid., pp. 606 ff.

74

pope and that the bishops derive their power through him.[1]
This is based on Mt 18. He finally concludes that there is
really only one immediate subject of infallible authority in
the church, the pope, and that although the magisterium of all
the bishops acting together can propose something to the faithful as infallible and to be believed, it is infallible because
of their communion and conjunction with the See of Peter and
not per se. He puts this forth as a "theological conclusion,"
not as a dogma.[2] A council acting without the approval of the
pope does not perform an act of the magisterium cui competit
infallibilitas.[3] If a council wished to teach without the pontiff, they could err, but God would never permit this to happen.

The pope is not bound, however, to follow the opinion or
advice of a council; and although he ought diligently to study
and investigate before pronouncing on a matter, this can be done
in many ways, not only through the bishops, but by himself, his
theologians or counsellors.[4] The certitude of his pronouncements does not depend on human study or inquiry but on "the
assistance of the Holy Spirit who assists the pope immediately."
This promise of assistance is absolute and not conditional on
any human effort. There is a guarantee of truth to what is
defined even if no human effort were made at all.[5] He makes a
distinction between "special" assistance which is given
"mediately" to lesser teachers subordinate to the supreme

---

[1]Palmieri, Thesis XIV, pp.447 ff; and Thesis XVIII,
pp. 513 ff.

[2]Ibid., p. 637. [3]Ibid., p. 648; Mazzella, p. 602.

[4]Palmieri, pp. 650, 648.

[5]Palmieri, pp. 639, 714, 714; Mazzella gives a somewhat
more positive statement of the function of human inquiry on
pp. 603-04.

magisterium, e.g., bishops, and specialissima assistance, "whose
necessary term is the immediate infallibility of the teacher
whom the Holy Spirit assists," that is, to the pope alone.[1]
This enhancing of the papal position vis-a-vis a council
is manifest throughout the work. He makes another distinction,
for example, between the magisterium authenticus simul et
infallibilis (pope) and the magisterium authenticus simpliciter,
per se fallibilis (bishops or council).[2] Or again, he says that
the definition of a council and that of the pope are not two
species of the game genus, but rather they differ only in mode,
since "the definition of a council is the definition of the
Roman Pontiff proposed in a more solemn manner."[3] And further,
he remarks that an ecumenical council is never simply necessary
although it can be useful and relatively necessary.

Palmieri's concern with the subject who exercises the
magisterium in the church focuses, as we have seen, on the pope
and council. He only mentions the Fathers and theologians in
passing, in contrast with Franzelin who was quite interested in
how we regard the teaching of the Fathers. For Palmieri,
"doctors" are part of the ecclesiastical magisterium because
they are declared to be so by the church but not part of the
authentic (authoritative) magisterium since they have no divine
mission. The teaching of the Fathers has authority from its
antiquity and from their own knowledge, but they too lack the
charism of infallibility and so are not part of the authentic
magisterium. In short, only those are really part of the magisterium who have the jus docendi.[4] Once again, the juridical
framework dominates.

---

[1]Palmieri, pp. 653-54. [2]Ibid., p. 667. [3]Ibid., p. 691.
[4]Ibid., p. 691.
[5]Palmieri, pp. 196-201.

76

The response of obedience on the part of the faithful to
the magisterium is also beginning to be of more interest.
Beside the "obedience of faith" due to any definition of a
dogma of faith, Palmieri is concerned with the level and quality
of assent due to pronouncements of the Roman Pontiff even when
he is not speaking ex cathedra. Since even then the pope speaks
with authority and not merely as doctor privatus, he is due
obsequium silentii, that is, he should not be publicly contradicted, nor the opposite doctrine defended unless he has
permitted discussion among Catholics: and he is due assensus
religiosus, that is, assent from a religious motive which is
not more than morally certain (i.e., error is not impossible,
only improbable) so that if there were reason for thinking
otherwise, one could suspend assent.[1] The pope is more than a
private teacher and will have the help of the Holy Spirit when-
ever he is teaching the faithful. This is not the charism of
infallibility, however. It should be noted that this interest
in the obedience due the Pontiff is still a subsidiary one for
Palmieri. It is a "scholion."

Although Palmieri says nothing very new about the magisterium there is, I think, a discernible shift in emphasis to a
more legalistic, juridical notion of the magisterium. The
categories that dominate his thought are those of power, jurisdiction, and authority, rather than those of truth, continued
incarnation, or Mystical Body. Authority and certitude are his
overriding interests. Authority is the principle of unity and
stability in any society and especially in the church since here
it is so by divine will. Authority is the basis of certitude
about those things necessary for salvation. There is greater
interest in the subject of authority, especially the supreme

[1]Ibid., p. 719.

universal authority. There is a down-grading of the function of the councils and the bishops in general on the basis of his fear of the specter of Gallicanism. Mazzella is less juridically oriented but does share Palmieri's concern with authority, the dominant position of the Roman Pontiff and the fear of Gallicanism. Palmieri attributes an almost magical, miraculous character to the magisterium, abstracting it as far as possible from any human limitations and making it something "supernatural."

Louis Cardinal Billot

From 1885 to 1910 the dominant name in theology at the Gregorian University was that of Louis Cardinal Billot. For several reasons he is, perhaps, the best known of the theologians with whom we are dealing, though he is not the most significant for the doctrine of the magisterium. His work was in the more speculative and metaphysical areas of theology. Hocedez has called his most outstanding work, the treatise De Deo uno et trino (1895) "a metaphysical poem, the poem of the Relation."[1]

Born in Sierck, France, on January 12, 1846, he received his education in Metz and Bordeaux and the major seminary in Blois where he was ordained in 1869. He entered the Society of Jesus on February 26 of the same year and spent his novitiate at Angers and Laval where he taught Scripture from 1871 to 1875. He preached at Paris and Laval and then taught dogmatic theology at the Catholic University of Angers (1879-82) and at the Jesuit scholasticate on the Isle of Jersey (1882-85). Leo XIII personally had him called to the chair of dogmatic theology at the Gregorian University in Rome in 1885 for the express purpose of promoting Thomism. He was a faithful follower of Thomas,

---

[1]Hocedez, Histoire de la Théologie au XIXe Siècle, III, 370.

exegeting not the commentators so much but Thomas himself, and
rediscovering or reapplying many insights that had been forgotten
or ignored.[1] Most of his works are subtitled, "A Commentary on
. . ." such and such a part of the Summa.

Billot became a consultor to the Holy Office in 1910 and
the following year was raised to the cardinalate by Pius X--an
honor he was later persuaded to renounce because of his
sympathies with the Action Française. His bête noir was not so
much Protestantism as Modernism and Liberalism. He fought the
idea that individual liberty is man's supreme good, nor was he
very enamoured of democracy.[2] His ideas and words can be found
in the encyclical which condemned Modernism, Pascendi dominici
gregis (Pius X, 1907), and his De Immutabilitate Traditionis
contra modernam haeresim evolutionismi is directed against Loisy.
It is this later work along with his De Ecclesia Christi (1898-
1910) that contains his views on the magisterium.[3] Although he
died on December 18, 1931, at Galloro near Rome, his influence,
particularly in trinitarian theology, the theology of grace, and
Christology continued to be felt through the 1950's. His De
Verbo Incarnato, for example, has gone through eight editions,
the last of which was in 1942.

I would agree with Bellamy that Billot does the best job
of the nineteenth century theologians of keeping distinct the

---

[1]Bellamy, La Théologie Catholique au XIXe Siècle, pp. 152
ff; Hocedez, Histoire de la Théologie au XIXe Siècle, III, 370-
71; J. Lebreton, "Son Eminence Card. Billot," Etudes, CXXIX
(1911), 514-25.

[2]A section of his De Ecclesia Christi (Question XVII) has
been translated into English, with Billot's approval, under the
title Liberalism: The Satanic Social Solvent, translated by
G. B. O'Toole (Beatty, Pa.: The Archabbey Press, 1922).

[3]His other works include: De Verbo Incarnato, 1892; De
Ecclesiae Sacramentis, 2 vols., 1894-95; Disquisitio de natura
et ratione peccati personalis, 1894; De Deo uno et trino, 1895;
De virtutibus infusis, 1901; Quaestiones de novissimis, 1902;
De inspiratione Sacrae Scripturae, 1903; De peccato originali,
1910; De gratia Christi, 1912.

apologetic and dogmatic aspects of the treatise De Ecclesia.[1]
The first part of his De Ecclesia Christi is apologetic--to show
the truth of the Roman Catholic church and the falsity of other
separated bodies.[2] The second part, more strictly dogmatic,
takes up the internal constitution of the church, and it is in
Question X of the second chapter on the powers of the church
that he discusses the magisterium. He does not differ significantly from his immediate predecessors, especially Franzelin
whom he cites frequently and at length, on the basic aspects of
the doctrine of the magisterium. If anything, he brings their
ideas to greater clarity and precision. He treats first of all
of the existence and nature of the magisterium, then its object,
the ways in which it can be exercised, the obedience due to it,
and finally, at greatest length, the subject, i.e., who
exercises it.

It is indicative of Billot's approach that he does not
begin his treatment of the existence and nature of the magisterium with the usual scriptural citations but rather with a
commentary on St. Thomas' Contra Gentes, 1, c.4.[3] Despite the
fact that the starting point is the difficulty men have in
coming to a knowledge of the truth because of their historic
condition, he focuses this difficulty in terms of an answer to
Protestantism, i.e., that the means of knowing what is to be
believed is not a spiritus privatus nor the individual study of
Scripture but the "authority of the living magisterium."[4] This
magisterium is the "power of authentically proposing and defining

[1]Bellamy, La Théologie Catholique au XIXe Siècle, p. 229.

[2]Louis Billot, De Ecclesia Christi (3rd ed.; Prati:
Giachetti, Filii et Soc., 1909), p. 25. (Hereinafter referred to
as Ecclesia.)

[3]Billot, Ecclesia, p. 351. [4]Ibid., Thesis XVI, p. 350.

revealed truth."[1] This power is only inadequately distinct from
the power of jurisdiction, distinct only in its formality, and
so intimately connected that the two can be considered as one.
He cites Franzelin, thesis V, in support of this position.[2]

Billot's most important contribution to the doctrine of
the magisterium is his clear identification of it with Tradition
and the regula fidei.[3] Tradition is the preaching of the
church; it is the preaching

> ab aevo in aevum continuatam per apostolorum successores
> sub charismate indefectibilitatis, illius revelationis
> quae de ore Jesu Christi, vel apostolorum eius, Spiritu
> Sancto dictante, primitus fuit accepta . . . [4]

That is, of course, the definition of the magisterium. This
preaching of the church or tradition taken in its formal sense
(i.e., precisely as such) is the regula fidei.[5] The distinction
between the remote and proximate rule of faith he maintains but
in a very different sense than that used by Franzelin, Palmieri,
etc. "Remote," for Billot, refers to historically and tem-
porally remote--what the preaching of the church was at some
time in the distant past. "Proximate" refers to what the
preaching of the church is at present.[6]

The object of this preaching (or the material content,
tradition in the passive sense of Franzelin) which was the
remote rule of faith for Franzelin, is in way a rule for Billot.[7]
The formality of a rule lies not in that which is believed, but

---

[1]Ibid., p. 333.   [2]Ibid., p. 338.

[3]Cf. Mackey, The Modern Theology of Tradition, pp. 22-28;
Michel, "Tradition," D.T.C., column 1342.

[4]Louis Billot, De Immutabilitate traditionis contra
modernam haeresim evolutionismi (4th ed.; Rome: Gregorian
University Press, 1929), p. 20. (Hereinafter referred to as
Immutabilitate.)

[5]Ibid., pp. 23, 30.   [6]Ibid., p. 33.

[7]Cf. supra, pp. 53-55.

in that which <u>directs</u> one in believing by proposing the object to-be-believed.[1] Hence, tradition in the active sense, or in other words the infallible magisterium, is the <u>regula fidei</u>.

What was not so explicit in Franzelin is brought to clarity in Billot--tradition, the teaching of the infallible magisterium, and the rule of faith are completely identical.[2]

Scripture exists as a help to this magisterium, as it were a "means of preserving the dogmas of revelation and a rich deposit from which doctrine should be drawn in preaching the faith."[3] Billot is still responding to the <u>sola scriptura</u> principle of the Protestants.

Also in response to what he considers to be the Protestant notion of tradition--that it is a purely human affair, "facts of history passed on in community"[4]--he asserts that the authority of tradition and, therefore, of the magisterium, comes not from the human ingenuity involved but from the divine assistance promised by Christ. This assistance he defines as:

. . . quaedam providentia dirigens magisterium et praecavens ne in proponendo revelationem olim factam, in declarando sensum eius legitimum, in explicando res implicite in ea contentas, in notando errores eidem adversantes, a veri tramite unquam deflectat.[5]

This means that the infallibility of the magisterium cannot be reduced to causes arising from the principles of human nature but only from the influence of God. This makes the infallibility absolute, not hypothetical, that is, not dependent on fulfilling any conditions, "but only this, that any doctrine proposed by this supreme magisterium, ought by that very fact be conformed

---

[1]Billot, <u>Immutabilitate</u>, p. 23, n. 1.

[2]Mackey, <u>The Modern Theology of Tradition</u>, p. 25.

[3]Billot, <u>Ecclesia</u>, p. 365; Billot, <u>Immutabilitate</u>, pp. 28-30, 32.

[4]Billot, <u>Immutabilitate</u>, p. 24.

[5]Billot, <u>Ecclesia</u>, pp. 373,646.

82

to truth, and have the character of inerrancy."[1] The authority
of God intervenes since God has commanded man to listen to the
church--"Who hears you, hears me."[2]

The divine assistance, however, does not exclude but
demands human industry. It imposes a grave obligation to
inquire diligently into the fonts of revelation. The source of
infallibility does not lie in this human effort, however.[3] The
cause of infallibility is the divine assistance, not the human
effort, and hence it is as easy for infallibility to be located
in one subject alone (i.e., the Roman Pontiff) as in a congrega-
tion of all the greatest minds of the church. It does not
depend on the collection of human wisdom for its exercise.[4]

While this infallibility may be absolute in the sense of
not depending on anything human for its effect, it is nevertheless limited to its proper object and cannot operate outside
these limits.[5] Billot does not contribute anything new to the
understanding of what is the proper object of the infallible
magisterium. It is primarily "things of faith and morals contained formally explicitly or implicitly in the deposit of
catholic revelation," and, secondarily, it extends to those
things which are necessary to preserve the deposit of revelation,
such as condemnations of propositions and dogmatic facts.[6] The
infallibility extends to determined formulas although one cannot
say that the deposit is contained in this or that specific set
of words.[7] Yet it is not the words but the "sense" of a dogma
proposed by the magisterium that is infallible and immutable.

---

[1]Billot, Ecclesia, pp. 371, 373. [2]Ibid., p. 425.
[3]Ibid., pp. 646, 683; Billot, Immutabilitate, p. 26.
[4]Billot, Ecclesia, p. 646. [5]Ibid., p. 370.
[6]Billot, Ibid., p. 392.
[7]Ibid., p. 402.

To keep just the words but change the sense would be heresy.[1]
The magisterial infallibility extends also to those facts which
it is necessary to know with certitude such as the canon of
Scripture, whether or not a certain council was ecumenical, and
even, Billot says, to the canonization of saints.[2]

Although Billot is more concerned with the "subjection"
or obedience due to the magisterium than his predecessors, he
really does not add anything in this area either. He maintains
the distinction found in Franzelin between "divine faith"--the
obedience due to things proposed by the magisterium as revealed
by God--and "ecclesiastical faith"--the obedience of mind and
will due because of the revealed authority of the magisterium
itself. This is owed to other things proposed by the magisterium
not as divinely revealed, but as defined and to-be-believed.
Again, he cites Franzelin as authority for this position.[3]

Besides the identification of the magisterium with
tradition the other significant development of the doctrine of
the magisterium on Billot's part was his almost exclusive
limitation of the subject of magisterial power to the Roman
Pontiff. We have seen how much emphasis Palmieri put on the
place of the Roman Pontiff. Billot carries this trend forward
to its logical conclusion. The entire third part of the De
Ecclesia is entitled De subjecto potestatis sive De ecclesiastica
hierarchia. In fact, the hierarchy means the Roman Pontiff.

The first point he makes is that, while there are two kinds
of power in the church--that of orders and that of jurisdiction
--there are not two hierarchies. Both powers are united in one

[1]Billot, Immutabilitate, p. 38. He does not define what
he means by "sense" but he gives the examples of heretics like
Sabellius, Arius, Nestorius, Pelagius and Berengarius who kept
the same words but changed the "sense."

[2]Ibid., Ecclesia, pp. 414 ff.

[3]Billot, Ibid., pp. 420, 427.

84

hierarchy, but jurisdiction does not follow *ipso facto* from the character of orders nor is the extent of jurisdiction determined by the nature of the orders.[1] The magisterium, as we have mentioned, is an aspect of jurisdiction rather than of orders.

In contrast to government in civil societies, power (which comes from God in both cases) is given immediately through Christ to his vicar and from him descends to others. It does not come mediately through the community which then designates someone to exercise the power on its behalf. He says:

> Quare potestas ibi via prorsus directa, a Deo in Christum, a Christo in eius vicarium, a Christi vicario in caeteros quovis praesules descendit, nulla alia persona sive physica sive morali in ratione causae mediae se habente.[2]

The church is not related to its head as a civil society would be to its prince, for Christ is the head of the church, and is its source and origin. His vicar has his authority from Christ, not from the community. This constitution of the church, since it was established by Christ and intended by him to perdure, cannot change or be changed. The church is a *civitas a Deo tota descendens, facta secundum exemplar illius coelestis Jerusalem quae in aeternum non commovebitur*.[3] The church, then, is a pure and perfect monarchy and this by divine institution. He also uses the image of the church as a *domus* or *aedificium*, a building of which Peter is the foundation stone that undergirds the whole structure--the *principium firmitatis*.[4] This is based on Mt 16:18 ff. and Jn 21:15-17, and is more of an argument than an exegesis. Billot concludes that these texts indicate that Peter was designated supreme and universal ruler having primacy of jurisdiction and complete and total ecclesiastical power.[5] He

[1]*Ibid.*, p. 486. [2]Billot, *Ecclesia*, p. 513.
[3]*Ibid.*, p. 515. [4]*Ibid.*, p. 526.
[5]*Ibid.*, pp. 526, 531-32.

offers the usual arguments to show that this power was intended
by Christ to continue in Peter's successors.[1]
The other apostles had equal power of orders and were
equal in regard to their special charism of establishing the
church of Christ, but all jurisdiction, either theirs or their
successors', descends from the fullness of Peter's pastoral
power. The jurisdiction of individual bishops over their particular churches is exercised purely as vicars of Peter in whom
alone is the supreme and universal authority.[2] Billot,
incidentally, maintains the distinction of Franzelin, between
the ordinary and extraordinary functions of the apostles, only
the former being handed on to their successors.[3]

It is this subordination and subjection of the bishops to
the Roman Pontiff that comes across most clearly and strongly
in Billot--far more so than in Franzelin, Palmieri or Mazzella.
It is the pope who is the subject of the magisterium rather than
the episcopal college as we have seen in his predecessors. After
establishing the primacy of the Roman Pontiff and its immutability[4] (adding nothing to Franzelin in the latter case), he says
over and over again that it is the pope alone who has ordinary,
immediate, truly episcopal power over all and every individual
church, over all bishops whether dispersed through the world or
in council.[5] At the end of the treatise he discusses the bishops
(de Episcopis)in nine pages and councils (De Conciliis) in
six pages. The entire discussion of the bishops is in terms of
jurisdiction--that they have ordinary and proper jurisdiction

[1]Ibid., pp. 549 ff.   [2]Billot, Ecclesia, pp. 551 ff.

[3]Ibid., pp. 554-55, including a long quotation from
Franzelin, De Traditione, Thesis XXII, par. 2.

[4]Billot, Ecclesia, pp. 574, 598.

[5]Ibid., pp. 563, 574, 681.

86

over their flocks;[1] that they are constituted by divine law, not
human law; that their jurisdiction, while full and complete in
itself, can be limited by the Roman Pontiff.[2]

The brief discussion of councils is in much the same vein.
What is most important and constitutive of an ecumenical council
is that it is convoked by the Roman Pontiff. Indeed, Billot
says this is the nature of an ecumenical council.[3] His conclusion is that there are not two subjects of supreme power and of
infallibility but only one. A council has it only ratione Summi
Pontificis whose authority informs conciliar edicts and decrees.[4]
Perhaps the most telling phrase is that "Bishops are pastors and
teachers with respect to the people, but sheep and disciples
with respect to the Pontiff."[5] Hence, the magisterium for
Billot is the papal magisterium.

His statement on the papal magisterium is that of Vatican I:

. . . the Roman Pontiff, when he speaks ex cathedra, that
is, when acting in the office of shepherd and teacher of
all Christians, he defines, by virtue of his supreme
apostolic authority, doctrine concerning faith or morals
to be held by the universal Church, possesses through the
divine assistance promised to him in the person of St. Peter
the infallibility with which the divine Redeemer willed his
church to be endowed in defining doctrine concerning faith
or morals; and that such definitions of the Roman Pontiff
are therefore irreformable because of their nature, but
not because of the agreement of the Church.[6]

He is, as he says, merely applying what he has previously said
about the powers of the church, its infallibility, the object
of this infallible teaching authority, to the Roman Pontiff as
the subject of this power. Then he explains what he understands
by each of the terms--that the pope must be speaking as a public
person, not as private theologian, to the entire church, not to
some local region, that definition implies a final and definitive

---

[1]Billot, Ecclesia, p. 691. [2]Ibid., p. 692.
[3]Ibid., p. 699. [4]Ibid., p. 704. [5]Ibid.
[6]Billot, Ecclesia, Thesis XXXI, p. 638; cf. also D.S. 3074,
T.C.T. 219.

dogmatic judgment, etc.[1] He says that popes can be infallible in encyclicals but that this is not the locutio ex cathedra of which the Vatican I canon speaks.[2] Billot says that it is easy enough to discern whether the pontiff is speaking ex cathedra or not by giving a series of examples where there is no doubt. Finally, he comes down to saying that we cannot set up conditions and then inquire whether or not the pope has fulfilled them any more than we could for a council. The only criterion is has he defined it or not:

> an de facto definiverit vel non definiverit, quia si definivit et in definiendo (ut supponitur) est infallible, ipsum definitionis factum secum necessario infert conditiones omnes quaecumque tandem illae sint, ad infallibilitatem requisitae.[3]

The very fact of definition carries with it all the necessary conditions for infallibility, whatever they may be.

Hence, for Billot, the only real subject of the infallible magisterium is the Roman Pontiff. Bishops may associate with a "judicial act of definition" if they are admitted to this by the pope,[4] and councils are only useful to add weight and solemnity which de facto does more to sway men but adds nothing to the intrinsic strength or validity of a pontifical decree.[5]

This exposition of Billot's notion of the magisterium—what it is, how it functions, who exercises it—is taken basically from the De Ecclesia Christi. There is nothing inconsistent with it nor added to it in the De Immutabilitate Traditionis, and we have cited the places where he says the same things, but this work is directed specifically against Loisy and his attempt to deal with the problem of history and dogma. Billot sees this as based on a false notion of tradition (or the

[1]Ibid., pp. 639 ff. [2]Ibid., p. 641. [3]Ibid., p. 645.
[4]Billot, Ecclesia, p. 681.
[5]Ibid., pp. 684-86.

magisterium),[1] which leads ultimately to a denial of revelation,
i.e., *verae et proprie dictae locutionis Dei*. It is founded on a
concept of relative truth and the application of the historical
method to tradition as if tradition were a plain and simple fact
of human history.[2] Such an application of the purely historical
method, prescinding from the higher (theological) criteria, in
interpretation of Scripture and tradition is not sufficient and
leads to heresy.[3] The historico-critical method is useful only
in the case of the *praeambula fidei*, but is "insufficient and
improportionate" when it comes to the sense and interpretation
of revelation and its source.[4] Here "higher" principles--the
special rules that pertain to revelation--the *criteria theolo-
gica*, must come in.[5] In contrast to this theological method,
as well as in contrast to the "method of immanence" of the
Modernists,[6] Billot says that the historical method generally
consists in two things: that it deals with texts, *monumenta*,
facts that are *external*, and that it employs only experimental
criteria which can be used by the *natural* faculty of human
reason.[7]

What Billot is interested in maintaining and what is
pertinent to our study here is the *immutability* of tradition or
of the magisterium. This is so because, in his mind, infallibility and immutability are very closely connected. If we admit

---

[1]Billot, *Immutabilitate*, pp. 7-8. [2]*Ibid.*

[3]Billot, *Immutabilitate*, pp. 96-97. [4]*Ibid.*, pp. 89 ff.

[5]*Ibid.*, pp. 90, 96-97. He does not say what these are.

[6]The "method of Immanence" Billot describes as "consisting
in demonstrating the religious truth, or the credibility of the
Christian faith, purely from the aspirations, exigencies and
energies which belong to the human spirit as such." *Ibid.*,
pp. 79-80.

[7]*Ibid.*, p. 80.

that the sense of the ancient church about some dogma of our religion was different than the sense of the church at present and that what is preached by the church today, may be corrected tomorrow, then it follows that the ancient tradition (read magisterial teaching) erred and that today's preaching may also err. For Billot, that is denial of infallibility and of the promise of Christ.[1] It is this difficulty that the notion of relative truth is intended to solve.

Billot's own attempt to come to terms with this difficulty is founded on a quite different model of truth which we will discuss at greater length in the following chapters. Briefly, it is the traditional scholastic definition found in St. Thomas in terms of conformitas intellectus et rei.[2] With this as a premise, his view of "development" is that there are three stages through which an individual dogma may pass--that of "simple faith," the state of perfect explicitation, and the intermediate state of transit from one to the other through theological speculation, a period of difficulties and ambiguities.[3] Any contradictions which may seem to appear between the earlier stages and the final precise explicitation are to be solved in terms of two principles to which he is willing to reduce this entire discussion: first, that texts of the Fathers or other sources of the tradition can be understood in an orthodox sense, and secondly, that they should be so understood. These are the principles which are the appropriate criteria of the catholic tradition.[4] "Orthodox sense" is the preaching of the magisterium at the present time--the regula fidei. For the underlying

---

[1]Billot, Immutabilitate, pp. 98-99.

[2]Ibid., p. 101. He cites Aquinas, S.T., I, q. 16, aa. 1-2.

[3]Ibid., pp. 46 ff.

[4]Ibid., p. 66.

90

premise of infallibility (and immutability) is that the church
cannot have taught in the past other than she is now teaching.[1]
If the Modernists answer that the positive data contradict this,
that only shows the error of their method of interpretation--
Billot calls it the "Protestant method."
Billot's explicitation of this close connection between
infallibility and immutability is most significant for understanding the theology of the magisterium of the Roman School.
It is a major factor in the current "crisis of authority."[2]

Timotheus Zapelena et al.

This was a period of growth for the Gregorian University
and the faculty expanded as well as the student body.[3] Although
Billot did not stop teaching until 1912, he had begun to teach
the more dogmatic tracts to second, third and fourth year
students and the first-year matter in which the magisterium was
treated was taken over in 1901 by Herman Van Laak.[4] He is listed
in the Gregorian Kalendaria for the period as teaching first-
year theology until 1911 when, for the first time, it is called
Fundamental Theology. He continued to teach this matter (with
one interruption, 1916-20) until 1928. For three years (1926-
28) he was joined in the area of ecclesiology by Joseph de

[1]Billot, Immutabilitate, pp. 43-44.

[2]It is interesting to note that the De Immutabilitate is
still on the shelves of the Gregorian University bookstore.

[3]There were 146 theological students in 1869, 400 in 1889,
648 in 1906, and 866 in 1928.

[4]Herman Van Laak was born in Rheinberg, Germany on August
23, 1866 and entered the Society of Jesus before his seventeenth
birthday. He was ordained in Rome and began teaching at the
Gregorian University in 1900. He was primarily a Bellarmine
scholar. His writing was almost entirely his notes for his
students and includes: Institutiones Theologiae Fundamentalis
(Rome, 1908-11), of which a brief summary was issued under the
same title in 1921-22; Theses quaedam de Patrum et theologorum
magisterio necnon de fidelium sensu (Rome: Gregorian University
Press, 1933).

Guibert whose main field was ascetical theology.[1] Neither added
or changed anything in the teaching of the magisterium from
their predecessors. Indeed, their textbooks are little more
than a reordering (for the use of their students at the
Gregorian) of the work done by Franzelin, Palmieri, Mazzella,
and Billot. They are the typical manualists, citing one
quotation from authority after another and putting arguments in
brief, logical form. To take them up individually is unneces-
sary and would again be intolerably repetitious. I will
indicate with passing references that they do say the same
things as Zapelena whose presentation will represent the latter
part of our period.

Timotheus Zapelena was born in the city of Elgarriagia in
Navarre on August 22, 1883. He studied at the seminary in
Pamplona and at the University of Salamanca and entered the
Society of Jesus before completing his theological studies on
November 9, 1903. He was ordained on July 30, 1917, at Oñia,
where he taught theology after completing a biennium in Rome.
He began teaching the tracts de Traditione, de Romano Pontifice,
and de Ecclesia at the Gregorian University in 1929. He pub-
lished his de Ecclesia Christi in 1930 and it was republished
six times, the last edition coming out in two volumes in 1954-55.
It was used as a text for the De Ecclesia course until 1961.[2]

[1]Joseph de Guibert was born on September 14, 1877, at Isle
nur Tarn in France and entered the novitiate of the Society of
Jesus at Toulouse in October of 1895. He studied at the Sorbonne
and at the theologate at Enghien, Belgium. He taught at the
regional seminary at Lecce, Italy and was a chaplain in the war
(1914-18). In 1920, he founded the Revue d'Ascetique et de Mystique and soon after began the Dictionnaire de Spiritualité. He
began to teach ascetical theology in 1922 and wrote his De
Christi Ecclesia in 1928. He died March 18, 1942.

[2]Timotheus Zapelena, De Ecclesia Christi (2 vols.; 6th ed.;
Rome: Gregorian University Press, 1954-55). His other writings
include the Summarium Theologiae fundamentalis (Oñiae, 1926),
and various articles.

92

The clear distinction made by Billot between the apologetic
and dogmatic treatments of the church was maintained by van Laak
and de Guibert but is expressed existentially by the time of
Zapelena, to the extent that another faculty member, Sebastian
Tromp, taught the tract De Ecclesia exclusively from the dogmatic point of view. Tromp did not treat the question of the
magisterium at all, but devoted his time to developing the
theme of the church as the Mystical Body of Christ.[1] Zapelena
himself proceeded on a continuum from the apologetic approach
at the beginning of his tract to the purely dogmatic mode at
the end.[2] His treatment of the magisterium comes in the
middle, however, and is both apologetic and dogmatic. His
presentation of the doctrine of the magisterium brings to
clarification and explicitation the positions and distinctions
that have been developing throughout the period we are treating
and serves well as the basis for our summation of the doctrine
of the Roman School.

Zapelena locates his Tractatus de Magisterio Ecclesiastico
(for the first time we meet it as a separate tract) after his
consideration of the jurisdictional power of the bishop. He
defines the authentic magisterium as the "public power of teaching, constituted by legitimate authority, to which there
corresponds in the hearers the obligation of accepting the
doctrine proposed."[3] He distinguishes four functions of this

[1]Sebastian Tromp, Corpus Christi quod est Ecclesia (2nd
rev. ed.; Rome: Gregorian University Press, 1946). There is an
English translation of this under the same title, trans. by Ann
Condit (New York: Vantage Press, 1960).

[2]Zapelena, De Ecclesia, I, 47. He explains the "dogmatic
method" by saying that it proceeds by way of authority--the
authority of God revealing and the church teaching but it comes
down to magisterial statements; the "apologetic method" proceeds
by way of critical inquiry, either historical, philosophical, or
exegetical, p. 45.

[3]Zapelena, De Ecclesia, II, 124; cf. also Joseph de Guibert
De Christi Ecclesia (2nd ed.; Rome: Gregorian Univ. Press, 1928).

magisterium in the church: 1) that of witness to the revealed
word of God, and 2) closely related to this, the function of
teacher--to explain and illumine the word of God, 3) that of
interpreter--since most of the "christian mysteries" are contained in Scripture, the function of teaching requires interpreting these writings, and 4) the function of judge, that is,
to make authoritative decisions when controversies arise because
of the obscurity and complexity of Scripture or because of
challenges to the deposit which the magisterium was constituted
to protect.[1]

His argumentation for the institution of such a magisterium
by Christ is based on the usual scriptural loci--Mt 28:18 ff,
Mk 16:15-16, Jn 20:21--and a series of Pauline texts indicating
the "divine mission" of preaching in the church.[2] He then gives
the "proof from tradition," citing texts from the early
Apologists and Fathers and then the rational arguments against
private interpretation and the sola scriptura principle of the
Protestants.

Infallibility Zapelena defines as the impotentia errandi,
excluding both the fact of error and its possibility. This
infallibility is a participated infallibility, however. This
means it is not the infallibility enjoyed by God himself, but is
dependent on Him and conditioned, restricted to a certain genus
of objects.[3] It is dependent on God's help and this help is
given in the form not of inspiration or revelation, but
"assistance," that is, a special direction of divine providence
by which God prevents error whether in the "teaching church" or

[1]Zapelena, De Ecclesia, II, 121-22.

[2]Rom 10:13 ff; I Cor 1:17; I Cor 4:1 ff; Rom 1:1 ff; II
Cor 10:4 ff; Gal 1:6 ff; I Tim 1:18 ff; Ephes 4:11 ff.

[3]Zapelena, De Ecclesia, II, 133; cf. also Herman Van Laak,
Institutiones Theologiae Fundamentalis, Tractatus IV, De Ecclesia
(Prati: Giachetti, Filii et Soc., 1911), pp. 32-36.

the "learning church." The infallibility in the teaching church
he refers to as "active"; that in the learning church he calls
"passive." Passive infallibility depends both on the assistance
of God and the teaching magisterium (active infallibility) but
active infallibility does not depend on the passive although the
ecclesiastical magisterium of a later age may use the passive
infallibility of the church of an earlier age as a criterion for
discerning revealed truth. He cites the dogmatic definition
of the Assumption of Mary as an example of this.[1]

His basic argument for infallibility in the magisterium
is the same as that of his predecessors, i.e., God could not
have obliged people to assent to the preaching of the church
under pain of loss of eternal life if that preaching could err.
He also says explicitly what Franzelin and Palmieri had suggested earlier (cf. supra., Ch.II), that the unity of the church
required this kind of teaching authority. He specifically cites
Jn 17:17--Christ's prayer for the unity of his followers--and
says that the apostolic magisterium would not be an apt means
toward this end unless it had the charism of infallibility.[2]
Christ prayed that they should be consecrated in truth and the
Spirit that was to come upon them is called the Spirit of Truth.
Those who teach and bear witness with this Spirit must be
infallible.

Zapelena's theological argument for the infallibility of
the magisterium is worth noting here because, once again, he
explicitates what has been underlying the reasoning of most of
the Roman School and that is that the church is indefectible
(cannot fail) in its existence as well as its essence, but it
would not be indefectible if it could err in matters of faith
and morals. The church's indefectibility implies immutability,

---

[1]Zapelena, De Ecclesia, II, 135.   [2]Ibid., 139.

and immutability implies infallibility.[1] This line of reasoning
we will discuss further in the next chapter.

The same biblical texts that are used to support arguments
for the infallibility of the magisterium are used to argue to
its perpetuity. His "dogmatic proof" is a series of citations
from magisterial statements--Vatican I, Leo XIII's Satis cognitum
and Pius XII's Mystici Corporis--thus exemplifying what he
understands by "dogmatic proof."[2]

Zapelena then reviews at length the discussion we have
mentioned previously as to whether or not the magisterium was
distinct from the power of jurisdiction. He cites the two
basic opinions--that the division of powers in the church is
only twofold, that of orders and that of jurisdiction (thus,
Palmieri and Mazzella), or threefold, that of orders, jurisdiction, and magisterium (thus, Franzelin and Billot in more
nuanced form) and inclines to the former himself. His point is
that the "divine mission" is a power formally juridical. The
teaching power in the church is not just a teaching power as in
a university, but the power of teaching authentically or with
authority to oblige assent. This is, therefore, "a public power
of ruling subjects in the doctrinal order."[3] It is this power
and intent of obliging assent that distinguishes the teaching
of the magisterium from the teaching of theologians who treat of
the same subject matter but without the right or purpose of
commanding assent.[4]

Zapelena begins his treatment of the subject of the

---

[1]Ibid., 142, I 221; De Guibert, De Christi Ecclesia, p. 70.

[2]Zapelena, De Ecclesia, II, 143-45.

[3]Ibid., 153, "est ergo potestas publica regendi subditos
in ordine doctrinali"; De Guibert, De Christi Ecclesia, p. 175.

[4]Zapelena, De Ecclesia, II, 158.

96

magisterial power with the statement that it is the bishops and
only the bishops who succeed to the power of the authentic
apostolic magisterium by divine right. He intends this to
exclude laymen (even *periti*), priests and pastors, but not the
pope who is obviously a bishop also. The others may share in
the teaching office of the church, but by delegation, as helpers
to the bishops, not by divine right. The bishops are the subject of the ordinary magisterium either taken by themselves in
their own dioceses or in local synods and this can sometime be
infallible; taken all together in an ecumenical council they are
the subject of the extraordinary and infallible magisterium; or
finally, the bishops collegially but not in council are the
subjects of the ordinary and infallible magisterium.[1]

The bishops have ordinary magisterial authority since they
have the power of jurisdiction of which the magisterium is a
part. This he has shown previously by historical evidence and
by dogmatic evidence.[2] The highest and most obvious form of
this episcopal magisterium is an ecumenical council which he
defines as a "legitimate assembly of the pastors of the whole
catholic church to deliberate and decide about affairs of the
universal church in order to produce decrees with the highest
authority."[3] Three things are involved in an ecumenical
council: convocation by legitimate authority, its "celebration"
which involves the questions of who should preside and who
should attend (both of these are matters of canon law with
difficulties not pertinent to our study), and confirmation by

---

[1] Zapelena, De Ecclesia, II, 171-72; De Guibert, De Christi
Ecclesia, p. 194.

[2] Zapelena, De Ecclesia, II, 7-19.

[3] Ibid., 175-76, "coventus legitimus pastorum totius
Ecclesiae catholicae ad deliberandum et decernendum de negotiis
Ecclesiae universalis ita ut decreta supremam auctoritatem
obtineant"; De Guibert, De Christ Ecclesia, p. 223.

the Roman Pontiff. This latter is absolutely necessary,
although it may precede, be concomitant with or subsequent to
the actual council.[1]

Not everything an ecumenical council says is to be considered infallible, however. That about which a majority of
the fathers pronounce definitively (peremptorie) in matters of
faith and morals is to be considered infallible.[2] This would
include the canon and that in a chapter which is definitively
proposed but not the obiter dicta, scriptural illustrations,
or speeches of bishops in the council, etc.

Besides this extraordinary magisterium, the bishops may
be infallible in their ordinary exercise of the teaching
authority. The same conditions for infallibility apply here
also--i.e., the bishops taken together (a majority), concerning
a matter of faith or morals, and with the approval of their
head, the Roman Pontiff, and definitively.[3] The distinction
between extraordinary and ordinary magisterium, says Zapelena,
lies not in the fact that the first is infallible and definitive
while the latter is fallible and provisory, but rather in three
other factors. First, extraordinary magisterium is exercised in
one place and after consultation and discussion among the bishops
and with advisors, whereas the ordinary magisterium is exercised
by the bishops dispersed throughout the world. Secondly, the
extraordinary magisterium occurs rarely, the ordinary can be
of daily occurrence; and thirdly the extraordinary is exercised
by the bishops personally while the ordinary magisterium may be
exercised through subordinates--parish priests, theologians,

---

[1]Zapelena, De Ecclesia, II, 179-80.

[2]Ibid., 181.

[3]Ibid., 184.

canonists, etc.[1] The two modes of exercise should not be
separated, however. The ordinary magisterium is a way of pre-
paring for and explaining the more solemn definitions of popes
and councils.

Besides the universal episcopate there is another subject
of the infallible magisterium which is, as it were, "the apex
and ultimate cause of all ecclesiastical infallibility," the
Roman Pontiff. He then goes through the definition of Vatican I
and explains each aspect--that the power is in each and every
person who is the Roman Pontiff, thereby excluding the distinction between _sedes et sedentes_, that he has it as a public
person, not as a private doctor, that he must propose a doctrine
with full authority as definitive and directed to the universal
church and that the intention of defining must be manifest.[2]
The papal infallibility extends to all those things to which
the church's infallibility itself extends. This, says Zapelena,
was the intention of the Council in using the words _ea_
infallibilitate pollere, qua divinus Redemptor Ecclesiam suam in
definienda doctrina de fide vel moribus instructam esse voluit
(DS 3074). The efficient cause of the papal infallibility is,
once again, the assistance of the Holy Spirit. He notes also
that this does not confer omniscience on the pope, but supposes
that he will not neglect the human investigation of the sources
of revelation.[3] In commenting on the _ex sese_ phrase, he distinguishes between the _existence_ of a consensus, which, he says,
is never absent, and the _causality_ of a consensus which is never
required.

---

[1]Zapelena, _De Ecclesia_, II, 187; De Guibert, _De Christi_
Ecclesia, pp. 300, 307.

[2]Zapelena, _De Ecclesia_, II, 194-95; De Guibert, _De Christi_
Ecclesia, p. 180.

[3]Zapelena, _De Ecclesia_, II, 196.

Although he spent as much time as he did (far more than any
of his predecessors) on the bishops as subject of the infallible
magisterium, he still makes the same comment about the relative
merits of councils as did Billot--they are not necessary, but
can be useful.[1]

When it comes to the object of the magisterium, Zapelena
is again clearer and more explicit than the previous members of
the School. The primary object are those truths revealed for
their own sake, which have innate importance for salvation--the
res fidei vel morum. The secondary object are those truths
virtually revealed, that is because of their connection with
the formally revealed truths. These can be of three varieties:
those connected logically, necessarily and consecutively with
the formally revealed truths, those related as presuppositions,
i.e., the praeambula fidei, and finally those that have a merely
external, historical, contingent connection--dogmatic facts.[2]
He says further that virtually revealed means those truths which
can be logically deduced by truly deductive reasoning, that is,
not introducing merely a new formula (ratiocinium mere
expositorium) but leading to a new concept in the conclusion,
or a new reality. Virtually revealed includes, he says, "everything which is deduced with logical and metaphysical necessity
from one premise formally revealed by God, the other naturally
certain," or, in other words, theological conclusions.[3] The
reason infallibility must extend to these virtually revealed
truths is that they are logically and metaphysically connected
with the formally revealed, so that the denial of the former
would imply the denial of the latter and the integrity of the

[1]Ibid., 217. [2]Ibid., 223-24.

[3]Zapelena, De Ecclesia, II, 230.

100

deposit of revelation would be lost. The same reasoning applies
to the extension of infallibility to the *praeambula fidei* and
dogmatic facts (historical facts needed to guard, propose or
apply dogmas).[1]

For Zapelena, the infallibility of the magisterium also
applies to words and phrases, since the charism of infallibility
implies the assistance of the Spirit in proposing as well as
understanding revealed dogma. But it is impossible to propose
dogma correctly without selecting words and phrases that convey
the meaning. Hence, the church must be able to decide which
words and phrases aptly express revealed truth.[2]

It is perhaps worth noting the argument Zapelena uses to
show that infallibility applies to dogmatic facts, canonization
of saints, disciplinary and liturgical laws as well as the
approval of religious orders. The argument is, first, that the
church knows the limits of her infallibility, second that she
has used it in these cases, and third, therefore it must be
legitimate matter for the exercise of infallibility.[3] Such
decisions are infallible, of course, only insofar as doctrinal
judgments are implied.

After giving a long exposition of the relation of the
magisterium to tradition according to Deneffe, Zapelena approves
it as his own with some slight modification. For Deneffe,
tradition in its principal meaning and strict sense is the
preaching of the faith by the living magisterium (he includes
both the act and the content--tradition active and passive) and
in a secondary and derived sense, tradition is the *monumenta*,

[1]Ibid., 234; De Guibert, *De Christi Ecclesia*, p. 280.

[2]Zapelena, *De Ecclesia*, II, 227.

[3]Zapelena, *De Ecclesia*, II, 238, 247, 253, 256.

the documents and records of that preaching.[1] Thus, Deneffe

identifies the magisterium with tradition. Zapelena's critique

is that there cannot be an adequate identification since, at

least in a secondary sense, the documents are tradition and

they are not the magisterium. Further, some of the persons who

actually do hand on the tradition, (e.g., Fathers and theologians)

are not themselves members of the hierarchy, i.e., not subjects

of the authentic and infallible magisterium.[2] Insofar as the

magisterium does produce documents itself, it can be a source

from which the magisterium of a later time draws and in this

sense can be said to be a fons revelationis.[3]

Zapelena is also clear on the position of Fathers and

theologians in regard to the magisterium. They are not subjects

of the power of teaching infallibly. However, under certain

conditions they can provide an infallible criterion of divine

tradition. These conditions are the same as those required for

the exercise of the infallible magisterium--a matter of faith

or morals, held strongly and definitively and with at least moral

universality.[4] The Fathers and theologians are so closely

associated with the magisterium that if they should err under

the conditions mentioned, it would be tantamount to saying that

the church could err. The Fathers, he says, are midway between

the "learning church" and the "teaching church," whose infal-

libility they share. Their writings are documenta secundaria

of tradition since they do not come directly from the authentic

---

[1]August Deneffe, Der Traditionsbegriff (Munster: Aschendorffsche Verlagsbuchhandlung, 1931), pp. 108-12.

[2]Zapelena, De Ecclesia, II, 277, as well as his article,
"Problema Theologicum," Gregorianum, XXV (1944), 38-73.

[3]Zapelena, De Ecclesia, II, 283.

[4]Zapelena, De Ecclesia, II, 289-90; De Guibert, De Christi
Ecclesia, p. 313.

magisterium but from authors who are in union and harmony with
the magisterium.[1]

Zapelena's presentation of the doctrine of the magisterium
is the finalized form of this doctrine in the Roman School.
The shape and lines that began with Franzelin, went through a
certain shift in emphasis with Palmieri and Billot, have become
clear and distinct in Zapelena. There was increasing concentration on the pope as the subject exercising this teaching power
in the church with a corresponding deemphasis on the role of
the episcopal college, increasing concern with authority as the
source of unity in the church and with the assent that this
authority could impose, and an increasingly juridical cast to
the doctrine as a whole. These were shifts in emphases only,
however. The basic arguments for the existence and necessity
of the magisterium as well as the understanding of its nature
and function in the church remained constant throughout the
period from 1870 to 1960. It is plain now that we are justified
in treating these theologians as a school.

We will explore the underlying presuppositions of this
doctrine in the form of paradigms in the following chapter.

---

[1]Zapelena, De Ecclesia, II, 285.

CHAPTER IV

THE PARADIGMS

We have presented the theology of the magisterium of the
Roman School, the theology which has formed the attitude of a
number of the hierarchy, the Curia, and recent popes, including
Paul VI. Now we wish to delineate the paradigms which are
operative in that theology. The notion of paradigm in the sense
developed by Thomas S. Kuhn is employed as mentioned above,
(page 5) only analogously. This chapter, then, will explain
Kuhn's theory and note the similarities and differences when
applied to theology. In the second part, we will explicitate
the paradigms that emerge from the theology of the magisterium
of the Roman School. The description of these paradigms may be
disputed in details, but the overall outline is clear from what
we have already seen.

Kuhn's Notion of Paradigms

A paradigm for Kuhn is the "universally recognized scientific achievements that for a time provide model problems and
solutions to a community of practitioners."[1] While a paradigm
in established usage is an accepted model or pattern which
functions "by permitting the replication of examples any one of
which could in principle serve to replace it," in science it is
rarely duplicated. "Instead, like an accepted judicial decision in the common law, it is an object for further articulation
and specification under new or more stringent conditions."[2]

---

[1]Kuhn, The Structure of Scientific Revolutions, p. viii.

[2]Ibid., p. 23.

Paradigms are shared by the community, and, indeed, "govern, in
the first instance, not a subject matter but rather a group of
practitioners."[1] It guides this group's research, defines its
problems, and suggests the means appropriate for their solution.[2] A paradigm is a vehicle for scientific theory--it tells
the scientist something "about the entities that nature does and
does not contain and about the ways in which those entities
behave." This is its "cognitive function. But it also has a
"normative" function, that is, it includes some "criteria for
determining the legitimacy both of problems and of proposed
solutions." These two functions go together. ". . . paradigms
provide scientists not only with a map but also with some of the
directions essential for mapmaking. In learning a paradigm the
scientist acquires theory, methods, and standards together,
usually in an inextricable mixture."[3]

In the Postscript in the second edition, Kuhn acknowledges
the vagueness and ambiguity of his use of the word "paradigm" in
the book and suggests that there are really two basic senses in
which it is employed. The first, more sociological meaning,
refers to the "constellation of group commitments"--"the common
possession of the practitioners of a particular discipline"
which is composed of "ordered elements of various sorts, each
requiring further specification." This use, he suggests, might
better be called the "disciplinary matrix." This group com-
mitment would include "laws" or symbolic generalizations," e.g.,
$f = ma$, "metaphysical paradigms," e.g., "all perceptible pheno-
mena are due to the interaction of qualitatively neutral atoms
in the void," and "shared values," e.g., quantitative

---

[1]Ibid., p. 180.

[2]Ibid., p. 103.

[3]Ibid., p. 109.

predictions are preferable to qualitative ones. Finally he
speaks of the component of the groups' shared commitments
"which first led me to the choice of that word," and which is
really the second and more proper use of the word, paradigm,
and that is, "exemplar," models--"the concrete problem-solut-
ions that students encounter from the start of their scientific
education, whether in laboratories, on examinations, or at the
ends of chapters in science texts."[1]

Although this second meaning of paradigm--the more specific meaning of exemplar or model--can be separated from the
broader "constellation of group commitments," it seems to imply
and be the basis for the other components of the wider notion
that he has mentioned. When explaining the second meaning, for
example, he says that the ability to see a variety of situations
as like each other, which results in a symbolic generalization
or "law," depends on solving a number of problems on the basis of
an "exemplary" problem-solution. The "shared values" and "metaphysical paradigms" are also dependent on the model or exemplar.
Thus, while Kuhn is willing after criticism to separate these
two usages of the term, the second is still part of the first
and wider usage, and the complexity contributes to the richness
and usefulness of the notion.

Kuhn's main thesis is that scientific knowledge has not
progressed in cumulative fashion, adding one insight and discovery to another, gradually building up a body of knowledge,
as is frequently imagined, but rather that the progress that has
occurred (and he does not doubt that there has been progress)
has been a series of "revolutions." These he defines as "a
displacement of the conceptual network through which scientists

---

[1]Kuhn, The Structure of Scientific Revolutions, pp. 181-87.

view the world,"[1] or, in other words, a shift in paradigms.
This is "a reconstruction of the field from new fundamentals,
a reconstruction that changes some of the field's most elementary theoretical generalizations as well as many of its paradigm methods and applications." He quotes Herbert Butterfield
as describing it as "handling the same bundle of data as before,
but placing them in a new system of relations with one another
by giving them a different framework."[2] With some caution, he
also suggests that the changes in visual gestalt is "a useful
elementary prototype for what occurs in full-scale paradigm
shift." At any rate, a scientific revolution is more than a
mere reinterpretation of data. All interpretation presupposes
a paradigm and interpretation only articulates the paradigm; it
does not change or correct it.[3] What Kuhn is describing is more
basic than that. It is a fundamentally different way of viewing
the world.

How does a shift in paradigms come about? First, it is a
process that takes time. It does not happen over night. It
begins with the recognition of "anomaly," i.e., "with the
recognition that nature has somehow violated the paradigm-
induced expectations that govern normal science."[4] Then follows
a period of extended exploration of the area of anomaly with
various attempts to fit it into the then-existing theory. Kuhn
points out that living with the awareness of anomaly for some
time usually produces a state of psychological disorientation

---

[1]Kuhn, The Structure of Scientific Revolutions, p. 102.

[2]Ibid., p. 85, n. 8. He cites Herbert Butterfield, The
Origins of Modern Science, 1300-1800 (London, 1949), pp. 1-7.

[3]Kuhn, The Structure of Scientific Revolutions, pp. 121-22.

[4]Kuhn, The Structure of Scientific Revolutions, pp. 52-53.
"Normal science" takes place when a paradigm is "in possession"
and the scientific community proceeds to solve the problems it
poses according to the criteria of solution it suggests.

and distress. When such an awareness of anomaly persists and penetrates a field of study "one can appropriately describe the fields affected by it as in a state of growing crisis." There is a "period of pronounced 'professional insecurity.'"[1] At the same time, other theories are put forward in an attempt to deal with the anomaly. A proliferation of theories, or versions of a theory, is a "very usual symptom of crisis." A new paradigm cannot take possession until it has first been compared with the older one and with nature itself. This testing of the paradigm occurs

> only after persistent failure to solve a noteworthy puzzle has given rise to a crisis. And even then it occurs only after the sense of crisis has evoked an alternate candidate for paradigm. In the sciences the testing situation never consists, as puzzle-solving does, simply in the comparison of a single paradigm with nature. Instead, testing occurs as part of the competition between two rival paradigms for the allegiance of the scientific community.[2]

The testing, however, is only a facet of the process by which one paradigm is chosen rather than another. Although he has been criticized as being subjectivistic (cf. Chapter V, page 146), he argues well that such decisions are not the coldly objective, factually provable ones the popular mind may attribute to scientists. Such decisions involve questions of standards and values which "can be answered only in terms of criteria that lie outside of normal science altogether, and it is that recourse to external criteria that most obviously makes paradigm debates revolutionary."[3] Kuhn speaks in terms of the "conversion" of the professional scientific group involved, of

---

[1]Ibid., p. 67.

[2]Ibid., p. 145.

[3]Kuhn, The Structure of Scientific Revolutions, pp. 110, 147-48.

108

a change in "allegiance."[1] It is, he says, ultimately a matter

of persuasion, not of mathematically objective proof. To quote

him again,

> Like the choice between competing political insti-
> tutions, that between competing paradigms proves
> to be a choice between incompatible modes of
> community life. Because it has that character, the
> choice is not and cannot be determined merely by
> the evaluative procedures characteristic of normal
> science, for these depend in part upon a particular
> paradigm, and that paradigm is at issue. . . . As
> in political revolutions, so in paradigm choice--
> there is no standard higher than the assent of the
> relevant community.[2]

The change that is being discussed is so fundamental that even

though the same words may be used by both sides of a paradigm

debate, communication is almost impossible, or, at best, "in-

evitably partial." Ultimately, it is sometimes the case that

a new paradigm achieves dominance only with the death of the

adherents of the older one.

There are other characteristics of the process of change

of paradigms which we will elaborate in the next chapter.

First, let us examine the paradigms involved in the doctrine

of the magisterium of the Roman School.

The Paradigms of Rome

As we have indicated, we are using Kuhn's analysis only

analogously and not making a literal transposition. There

are obvious differences between theology and the natural

sciences of physics and chemistry from which he takes most of

his examples. Theological models cannot be quantified nor can

their expression be reduced to mathematical formulae. Neither

---

[1]Ibid., p. 151.

[2]Ibid., p. 94. The applicability of this point to a
theological crisis we will discuss in the following chapter.

are theological models the basis of repetitive problem-solving,
nor are they mechanical models, although some treatments of
"grace" have come perilously close to this. Nonetheless, there
are paradigms operative in theology, as there are in the social
sciences.[1]

In this study, I will be using paradigm in both of the
senses Kuhn mentions--that broader notion of "disciplinary
matrix" and the more specific part of that wide sense, i.e.,
model or exemplar. In the case of theology, paradigm is not a
model problem-solution, but a conceptual model shared by a
group of theologians implying certain metaphysical pre-supposi-
tions and value-judgments as well as determining the questions
to be asked and the methods of solution (cf. page 104).

In the case of the doctrine of the magisterium, there are
both paradigms specific to this doctrine itself and paradigms
that underlie the entire theology of which this one doctrine is
only a small part. Three basic paradigms are involved in the
theology of the magisterium--that of the socio-political structure of the church, that of authority within that structure, and
that of truth and its mode of communication (teaching), which
for the sake of brevity, we will refer to as the epistemological
model. On the basis of the exposition in Chapters II and III,
we will attempt to describe these paradigms and their
implications.

First, the model of the socio-political structure of the
church was clearly that of a monarchy, of a kingdom, and,
indeed, as they stress, a pure monarchy, not a constitutional
one. The supreme and ultimate power is not divided between the

[1]Kuhn's theory has also been used to some extent in the
social sciences. For example, David Easton, "The New Revolution in Political Science," and Sheldon S. Wolin, "Political
Theory as a Vocation," both in The American Political Science
Review, LXIII, 4 (December 1969), 1051-61, 1062-82, respectively.

monarch and some other legally constituted body. It is given
directly by God to the supreme ruler, not mediately from God
to the people or the community as a whole who then delegate the
king to rule over them.[1] This is well summarized by Franzelin
in Thesis X:

> Christus Jesus regnum suum in terris ita instituit, ut
> tum in proxima praeparatione Matth. XVI. Luc. XXII tum
> in respondente illi exsecutione Jo. XXI <u>unum</u> Simonem
> Petrum ex ceteris et super ceteros Apostolos elegerit,
> quem potestate instruxit suprema et universali tum
> super singulas partes et singula membra Ecclesiae tum
> super totum corpus Ecclesiae; quae quidem potestas sit
> vicaria a Christo derivata, immediate immediatione
> virtutis in totum et in partes, plena quoad objectum
> proprium regni coelorum in terris. Propterea hoc ipsa
> potestate constituitur principium formans et continens
> visibilem unitatem Ecclesiae ex ipsa institutione Christi
> fundatoris ac jure proinde divino.[2]

This kingdom is not just like any other earthly kingdom,
but is the kingdom of heaven on earth. It is the kingdom of
truth and holiness.[3] It is more than a merely natural society;
it is a supernatural society--the communion of saints. Indeed,
this kingdom shares the qualities of the divine; it is united
with the divine. It bridges the gap between the divine and
human and is described frequently by the hyphenated phrase,
<u>humano-divina</u>. The Mystical Body ecclesiology with its close
identification of the Head and Body, instead of leading to a
more organic notion of the structure of the church as it has in
the Tübingen School, led to the <u>juridical</u> identification of the
human society with the divine. The church was the continuation
of the Incarnation, the uniting of the human and the divine on
earth.[4] Who hears the church, hears Christ. The same obedience due to Christ is due also to the "legates of God." An

---

[1]<u>Supra.</u>,"Franzelin," "Palmieri;" Franzelin, <u>Divina
Traditione,</u> pp. 103 ff.

[2]Franzelin, <u>De Ecclesia</u>, p. 124.

[3]<u>Ibid.</u>, pp. 47,77,379.

[4]<u>Supra</u>, Ch. II, "Perrone."

attack on the authority of the church is an attack on Christ himself. The communicatio idiomatum that applied between the two natures of Christ is now applied between Christ the head and the church, his body.[1]

Though it is a monarchy and a divinely affiliated one at that, there are others who have authority derived through the supreme ruler and subordinate to his. There are two orders in this society--those with authority and those without, superiors and subjects, rulers and ruled.[2] This arrangement was established by God through Christ and cannot be changed by man. The distribution of power is by divine will. Those who exercise this power, the bishops, are nonetheless subordinate to the supreme rule, the pope.[3]

In this kingdom, the function of authority is obviously of major importance, and so we come to the paradigm of authority in the Roman School. The more-than-human character of this authority is clear from what was said above about the close identification of the human structure with the divine. This authority is the very foundation of the church.[4] It is the basis of unity and universality, two essential qualities of the church of Christ. In this mode, unity depends on subordination. There could be no unity unless all are properly subject to some authority--the people to their bishops, the bishops to the pope (presumably, the pope to Christ, Christ to God the Father). The authority is given in the reverse order--all authority in heaven and on earth is given by God to Christ, Christ passes his authority on to his apostles but to Peter in particular.

---

[1]Supra, Ch. II, "Passaglia-Schrader."

[2]Supra, Ch. III, "Palmieri-Mazzella."

[3]Supra, Chs. II, III.

[4]Supra, Chs. II, III ; Franzelin, De Ecclesia, pp. 148, n. 1, 383.

112

The paradigm is that of a pyramid whose peak pierces the heavens
and beyond.

Because authority is the basis for unity, it is also the
basis for the universality of the church. This kingdom is meant,
intended by its founder, to extend to the entire world, to be a
universal kingdom. If it is to be one kingdom, there cannot be
a series of discrete but disconnected satrapies. The authority
of the kingdom is that which holds it together no matter how
dispersed it is geographically, and that which enables it to
extend itself universally.[1]

For these theologians, authority is the basis of order and
stability. Order means subordination of lower to higher; each
thing in proper hierarchical arrangement. This must be clear
and certain and unchanging. Then we have stability. There is
no place in this paradigm for change, uncertainty, probability
or open-endedness. That would mean disorder and instability,
and these are definitely negative values in this paradigm.

The source of this authority itself is a special gift of
God--the charism of truth (in the case of teaching authority).
This guarantees that the possessors of this charism accurately
preserve and propose the truth that has been given to them, and
thus they have authority. But the authority is not just the
power of the truth to compel the human intellect; it is the
authority to command, to impose an obligation, to compel
assent. It is founded on the premise that God wills all men to
be saved by their acceptance of the truth He has revealed to
some. To those few appointed ones and the ones they in turn
appoint to succeed themselves, He also gave the power to command and rule in His name. Thus, as we have seen in the preoccupation with the dispute about whether the potestas docendi

---

[1]Supra, Chaps. II, III;   Franzelin, Divine Traditione,
p. 44.

was part of the <u>potestas</u> <u>jurisdictionis</u>, the underlying concept
of authority was a juridical one, not one of moral force or of
intellectual persuasion. The authority did not depend on the
ability of the truth to convince, but on the legal right of the
bearers of authority to command. And so a great deal of time
and energy was expended to show that these were the legal heirs
who had validly and legitimately succeeded to the authority. If
this could be assured, then one need not further concern oneself
with the truthfulness of what they taught. That was guaranteed
by the legality of the authority. God had provided this safe
and certain means by which all men might come to know him and
his Word. The only other alternative, Franzelin says, would be
that the truths of faith could be scientifically demonstrable to
all, and this is patently impossible.[1] Underlying these statements is the paradigm of truth to which we now turn.

Their paradigm of truth was, as they so often referred to
it, the "deposit" model. The truth (they would say truth<u>s</u>) of
revelation were given complete, unified, consistent, absolute
and immutable from the beginning. They were laid away in what
was constantly referred to as the "deposit of revelation" and
handed out gradually as occasion demanded or challenge required.
Truth was something static and objective; it did not change or
grow. It just lay there waiting to be discovered and presented.
It was unified and consistent, for truth must be one just as God
who is truth itself is one. There can be no contradictions or
inconsistencies in God, nor can there be in truth. It was complete from the beginning, for, since revelation closed with the
death of the last apostle, all that we needed to know for salvation had to be given by that time.[2] The church knew it all,

<hr>

[1]<u>Supra.</u>, Ch. II, "Franzelin."

[2]<u>Supra.</u>, Ch. III, "Palmieri and Mazzella."

whether or not she realized it.

This truth was absolute in the sense that it depended on
nothing besides the fact that God had revealed it. It was not
dependent on the human mind of the knower or the teacher. God
saw to it that man did not interfere; even though human study
and investigation were needed, they did not affect the truth.
Men were instruments in the hands of God, but they could not
thwart His designs. In this respect, the charism of "assistance" was similar to that of revelation and inspiration, though
they were carefully distinguished. "Assistance" was not the
communication of new truths; it was merely the assurance that
previously given truths would not be lost or distorted. (Supra.,
pp. (cf. Chapter II, Franzelin).

Last but by no means least, truth was immutable. It could
not be added to nor diminished because it is divine and perpetual.[1] Just as God cannot change, neither can His truth. To
change from one form to another would be to say that the earlier
form had been wrong. But that is a contradiction in terms:
truth, especially divine truth, cannot be untrue. Hence, if it
was ever true, it must always be true.[2]

The basic paradigm of truth operative for these theologians, as we mentioned briefly earlier,[3] was the "scholastic"
understanding of truth. Although there are various mutants of
this theory, there is sufficient consistency to draw a paradigm
that may be accurately so described. The "consecrated definition from the philosophia antiqua," as Billot puts it, is the
adaequatio intellectus et rei, the conformity between thing

---

[1]Supra., "Billot"; Franzelin, Divina Traditione, p. 180.

[2]Supra., "Billot."

[3]Billot, Immutabilitate, pp. 101 ff.; Franzelin, Divina
Traditione, pp. 584 ff.

(an object in the world) and the human mind. The thing known is represented in the mind of the knower and to the extent that the representation is accurate, to that extent it is true. There were disputes about the process by which this representation takes place--some giving more emphasis than others to the activity or passivity of the intellect but all concerned with how something that existed "physically," "really," extramentally could also exist "intentionally," "conceptually," in the mind. Generally, the assumption was that the intellect was made for truth, ordered to it, but had to be "moved" from "potency" to "act." When the intellect was activated and was conformed to the object there was truth. This only took place, properly speaking, in an act of judgment. By this was meant not merely the mental activity of knowing what a thing was (simple apprehension -the concept of a man), but an act of comparing one concept with another, e.g., man is a rational animal, or an existential judgment, e.g., this object that I perceive is a man. In this act there could be conformity or disconformity of the intellect with the object concerned, i.e., there could be truth or falsity.[1] The underlying "concrete" model was that of matching diagrams or congruent triangles--if one matched the other exactly, there is truth. Only it was less empirically verifiable than that image would suggest, for what was being matched or "compared," to use Aquinas' word, were concepts existing in the mind with concepts (essences) of objects existing in the extramental world.

This brings us to another one of the major underlying paradigms operative in this view of the world and of truth, namely, that there were immutable essences that were knowable by man. An essence or nature (to use the scholastic terminology)

[1]Franzelin, _Divina Traditione_, p. 586.

is "that which makes a thing to be what it is," or "that which
determines a thing to be this thing and not something else."
Should an essence or nature change, the object would be some
other object and no longer what it was. This sounds rather
tautological perhaps, but it is the basis of the assumption that
what is true is immutable--veritas autem manet una et eadem in
aeternum.[1] If the essences (and things pertaining to the essence)
cannot change, and if one has true knowledge of it, then that
truth can never be otherwise. Hence, Billot could make no sense
out of any notion of relative truth--of such he says, ". . . you
are joining words without sense, making an empty noise, and you
do not understand what you are saying."[2]

That is why the only possible way for the Roman School to
understand progress or development was in terms of growth in
clarity or explicitness. There was no way for them to understand how something could be true in a certain context or framework but not in another. It was inconceivable in this paradigm
for a concept of "nature" or "person," which expressed truth
about the relation of Jesus Christ to God the Father, ever to
convey falsity about that relationship. For, once the mind was
in conformity with an essence, there was truth, and it could
never be otherwise. The most that could happen is that we would
come to a clearer, more distinctly grasped knowledge of that
essence. What once was known obscurely, could later come into
the light of clarity, but the essence did not change and the
knowledge of it, its intentional existence in the mind did not,
could not change. Immutable essences are the basis of immutable
truths.

The assumption that the essentialia were immutable was

---

[1]Ibid., p. 180.

[2]Billot, Immutabilitate, p. 106.

also the underlying reason for infallibility. Doctrines pertaining to faith and morals contained in the deposit of revelation were of the essence of the church. Hence, if they were not to be lost, or rather, if Christ had promised that they would not be lost or diminished, it is necessary that the church be infallible in preserving and proclaiming them. If the church could err in the essentialia, then she would cease to be the church. As we mentioned earlier,[1] infallibility follows from immutability and the immutability is the immutability of essences.

The other major characteristic of their paradigm of truth was that of certitude (the exclusion of doubt). Just as essences were, by definition, metaphysically unchangeable, so a true knowledge of such essences was absolutely certain. There were a number of ways in which error could be introduced into the process of knowing, but it was possible to achieve true and certain knowledge of objects existing outside the mind of the knower, and this was the ideal type of knowledge. It was to be expected that the things that were most important for a man to know, could be known with certainty, and the things pertaining to man's eternal salvation surely fall into that category. We have seen the argument for an infallible magisterium in the claim that God could not oblige a man to assent to something that he could not know with certainty, or that he could be in doubt about. Absolute, unqualified certitude was not only possible; it was the highest form of knowledge.

It was precisely this quality of certitude that the magisterium added to the truths of faith held and handed down in the community.[2] The source of the certainty was not the intrinsic

---

[1]Supra., "Billot."

[2]Palmieri, p. 48.

truth of the propositions which compelled the believer to assent
without doubt, but the authority of those who proposed the
things to be believed. It seemed necessary and fitting that the
"truths of faith" be known with as much surety as the truths of
science and mathematics. The clear, distinct and indubitable
proposition of the rationalist-Certesian model was the ideal
form of truth. The truths necessary for man's eternal salvation surely must be of this level. But the only means by which
this kind of knowledge of revelation may be had by mankind universally for whom it is intended is by authority. Thus, certain
knowledge requires authoritative teaching.

Thus far we have described the "cognitive" aspect of the
paradigms involved in the doctrine of the magisterium in the
Roman School. But besides this "content," the paradigms also
have a "normative" function. By this Kuhn means that the paradigm implies some criteria which determine what are considered
data, what problems are to be solved and the methods to be used
in their solution.

The data suggested by the paradigms just described were
all authoritative and from the past. Scripture, the writings of
the Fathers and the early theologians were considered "theological data." Personal experience, the sense of the contemporary
Christian community, or the problems of the society in which
they lived, were not considered data for theology. The truths
of the faith were to be sought by searching ancient writings,
for antiquity was a criterion of authority, and authority was
the basis of a certain knowledge of truth. By the time of
Billot, as we have seen, after Leo XIII's effort to revive
Thomism, Thomas himself became data for theology and, to a
lesser extent, other scholastic theologians of the thirteenth
and seventeenth centuries.[1] These too were used as authorities,

[1]E.g., Suarez, Bellarmine, Petau, Thomassin.

sometimes were repeated verbatim, sometimes cited as proof for a position. Data from other scientific or humane disciplines were not considered matter for theological reflection, except insofar as they could be used in the praeambula fidei. Revelation could be found in no place save the monumenta christiana.

However much the paradigms dictated that the theological data be taken from the past, the method of organizing and uti-lizing the data was not scientific or critically historical. The interest in the Fathers evidenced in Perrone, Passaglia and Schrader was limited to recovering the texts and using them (in the original when possible) as the basis for deductive reasoning or as proof-texts for dogmatic positions already held. In the latter part of our period, there was less concern even for this, and the citations from Perrone, Passaglia, Schrader and Franzelin were merely repeated with perhaps a bit more logical organization (Van Laak and De Guibert, for example.)

We have described Billot's understanding of the "histori-cal method"[1] which he maintained should be used only with respect to the praeambula fidei, not in elaborating revelation. In the latter case, higher "theological" principles take over. Two examples of this recur constantly in connection with the treatment of the magisterium: the problem raised for the doc-trine of papal infallibility by the condemnations of Pope Vigilius (Council of Constantinople, 553) and of Pope Honorius I (Council of Constantinople, 681, and confirmed by subsequent popes) where the facts, as far as can be determined by histori-cal criteria seem to contradict the dogmatic position;[2] and with regard to the question of what constitutes an ecumenical council,

---

[1]Supra., "Billot."

[2]E.g., Mazzella, pp. 866 ff; also Hans Küng, Infallible? An Inquiry, trans. by Edward Quinn (New York: Doubleday & Com-pany, Inc., 1971), pp. 114 ff.

120

the proposition that it must be convoked or at least approved by
the pope is contradicted by the historical facts. The theologians of the Roman School dealt with these conflicts of fact with
dogma on the assumption that what is certainly true is the theological position, and then any conflict is to be resolved by a
reinterpretation of the historical facts or by their correction,
not vice-versa. The primacy of fact over concept is described
by Billot as the "Protestant method."[1] The paradigms of authority and truth have dictated the data and the method of handling
the data.

The paradigms also influence the type of problems with
which the discipline occupies itself, as well as the methods of
solution to be employed. The two examples given above to illus-
trate the method of treating the data, also illustrated the
paradigm's influence on the kinds of problems raised. The problems tended to be ones of conceptual clarification and refinement, attempts to accommodate the logical definitions to the
historical facts when they seemed to disagree with the truths
that had been deduced from revelation. They could not define a
council as ecumenical because it had been convoked by the pope,
when historical research showed clearly that some councils,
which all wanted to designate as ecumenical, had not been so
convoked. In the face of this dilemma, the definition was modi-
fied to include subsequent approbation. The clearest example of
this type of problem was the discussion that lasted all through
the period concerning the relationship of the potestas docendi
to the potestas jurisdictionis. This had nothing to do with any
exegetical difficulty, nor anything in the experience of the
Christian community. The data and the method was strictly in
the conceptual order. In Zapelena's summary discussion of this

---

[1]Billot, Immutabilitate, p. 24.

matter, all the evidence was quotations from authorities, i.e.,
previous theologians.[1]

The same can be said of the discussion of whether or not
tradition and the magisterium should be identified or clearly
distinguished. They juggled definitions, stressing one aspect
or another, and on the basis of the logical relation of the concepts in use came to a conclusion. It reflected something of
their thinking but it had nothing to do with the Christian
experience nor with the daily life of the community. The problem was suggested by their paradigms of authority and of truth,
and the method of solution was also implied by those models.

Insofar as the model of authority was a juridical one
rather than a moral one, and insofar as the paradigm of truth
was that of the conformity of the concept to the extramental
essence, the problems were necessarily of a conceptual nature,
and the solution was the manipulation of immutably fixed concepts. The result was a narrowing of what was considered
"theology." By the end of our period the theological problems
were all clearly defined, and the possible opinions neatly laid
out. The anomaly came from the fact that no one but the theologians had these problems, and whatever option a theologian chose,
it made little or no difference in the life of the Christian
community. The authority of the magisterium was not enhanced by
the theological position that it was a part of the potestas
jurisdictionis. The attempt to compel obedience did not make
any proposition more truthful, nor did it appear so in the minds
of the members of the Christian community. The anomaly has
arisen from the fact that the magisterium no matter how it was
defined conceptually or juridically justified, became a less and

[1]Supra., "Billot."

less effective teaching instrument.[1]

Thus far we have described the cognitive content of the
paradigms underlying the doctrine of the magisterium in the
Roman School and the normative function these paradigms had in
determining the data, the problems and the methodology involved
in their solution. This descriptive task is our main purpose in
this chapter, but the question of how and why these particular
paradigms emerged and not some others naturally follows. To
answer this fully is beyond the scope of this study and would
require a book in itself, but a few general indications may be
given.

There are, of course, many approaches and aspects from
which to handle such a question in the history of ideas. The
psychological study of the theologians in question would be one
level of explanation. For lack of time, data, and expertise, we
will forego that. Further, since we are dealing with only one
doctrine of a school of theologians rather than with the whole
theology of an individual, a more sociological level of explanation seems warranted. We had hoped at the beginning of this
research to be able to show clearly the connection between the
paradigms involved and the intellectual and cultural milieu of
Western Europe during this period. That is always a difficult
business, and it is seldom possible to come to any demonstrable
conclusions. In our case it is doubly difficult, for there are
two "cultures" involved--that of Western Europe and that Roman
ecclesiastical milieu that has been designated Romanitas.
Although there were exceptions (Passaglia and Billot), the theologians who taught at the Gregorian University during our period
were more immersed in the peculiar ecclesiastical culture of

---

[1]Supra., 2,   and infra, Chap. V,especially Küng's
remarks cited there.

Rome than in the milieu of the countries from which they came or in the more general intellectual world of Europe as a whole. Nonetheless, Rome and the rest of Europe are not completely distinct, nor were their cultures. The events in Europe in the early part of the nineteenth century had had a profound effect on the "Roman world." The "revolution," in the extensive meaning that Kenneth Scott Latourette gives it, dominated the thinking of the period. This revolution really dated from the Renaissance and the Protestant Reformation, but its most impressive dates as far as Rome was concerned were probably 1789 and 1848--the French Revolution and the invasion of Rome by French forces. If I may quote Latourette:

> The revolution had many facets and eventually affected all aspects of civilization. They were in the realms of ideas, politics, religion, industry, transportation, agriculture, and economic theory, and in the accompanying changes in social structure. They included the widening of men's horizons on the age of the earth, on the structure of matter, and on the dimensions of the universe in which man finds himself. They led to a progressive emancipation of man's mind and included a humanitarian concern for the welfare of man and hope for improvements in that welfare. In these particular years the forms which the revolution assumed were chiefly political and into them entered philosophical and political theories.[1]

In the political sphere, the revolution was marked by the growth of liberal democracy and the trend toward a secularized state; in the economic and industrial spheres, the industrial revolution and the increasing mastery of man over his physical environment caused new problems in men's lives for which the church seemed ill-prepared, and which seemed to make religion increasingly less necessary. The scientific revolution and the application to the Bible of historico-critical methods posed

---

[1]Kenneth Scott Latourette, <u>The Nineteenth Century in Europe</u>, Vol. 1 of <u>Christianity in a Revolutionary Age</u> (New York: Harper & Brothers, Publishers, 1958), p. 203.

threats in the realm of religion itself.[1] All these aspects of
the revolution must be considered the horizon against which to
view the paradigms that emerge from the theology of the Roman
School. The challenges to authority in all realms had upset the
traditional order and attacked the church's position, property
and prestige. It is not surprising then, that the desire for
order and unity should lead to a stress on authority in both the
secular and ecclesiastical realms. They saw the rejection of
the church's authority in the Protestant Reformation paralleled
in the secular sphere by rejection of the authority of the
monarch.[2] Monarchy had been the form authority had taken in the
past and it was still in their minds the mode of exercise of
authority that brought about order and unity.

The doubts raised in the sphere of religion itself by such
scientific studies as Charles Lyell's Principles of Geology
(1830 and revised editions until 1872) and Charles Darwin's
Origin of Species (1859) understandably enough gave rise to an
increased desire for certainty in religious matters and an
increasing despair of man's ability to achieve it by his own
powers.[3] Despite the general optimism about man's ability to
dominate his environment and achieve certainty about the physical structure of his world, progress in scientific knowledge
seemed to breed more doubts than certainties when it came to

---

[1]Ibid., p. 232; H. D. McDonald, Theories of Revelation:
An Historical Study 1860-1960 (London: George Allen and Unwin,
Ltd., 1963), p. 78.

[2]Yves M.-J. Congar, "L'ecclesiologie, de la Revolution
française au Concile du Vatican, sou le signe de l'affirmation
de l'autorité," Revue des Sciences Religieuses, 1960, XXXIV, 77-
114; J. L. Altholz, The Churches in the Nineteenth Century (New
York: Bobbs-Merrill Co., Inc., 1967), p. 2.

[3]For a summary of the threat posed by the growth of scientific knowledge, see C. J. H. Hayes, Contemporary Europe Since
1870 (New York: Macmillan Co., 1953), pp. 187-220, 519-528; and
Latourette, The Nineteenth Century in Europe, pp. 216-222.

religion. It is not surprising that the paradigm of knowledge should be one which stressed authority, antiquity and certainty rather than empirical evidence, newness and hypotheses.

The relation between the paradigms of the theology of the magisterium at the Gregorian University and the general cultural climate of Europe at the time needs to be investigated much more than is possible here. But the possibility of establishing clear and direct relationships will always be severely limited by the insulation of the second cultural milieu of which we have spoken--ecclesiastical Romanitas. This particular atmosphere is difficult to describe to those without experience of it. The net effect is to elevate ecclesiastical and theological concerns way above their significance for the rest of the world. It is a very closed, self-sufficient world centered around the papal court. Like any government center, this social world is determined in large part by the power structure in the government, and the entire intellectual milieu is preoccupied with "affairs of state." In the case of Rome, those affairs were described in theological terms. That is not to say that there were only political issues described in theological jargon. There were serious theological issues involved, but it is difficult to extricate the one from the other.

Within this ecclesiastical context then, the paradigms were to some extent formed in reaction to specific theological movements. We have seen these in the textual study in Chapters II and III. In the early part of the period and continuing more in the background right up until Vatican II, the ogre in the theological forest is Protestantism. The apologetic case we have referred to was directed toward showing the identity of the Roman Catholic Church and its magisterial power with primitive

126

Christianity in response to the Protestant critique.[1] Hence,
the emphasis on antiquity as a criterion of truth. This was the
common ground on which the argument with the Protestants could
be fought. Also the rejection of papal authority by sixteenth
century Protestants seemed to be linked with the rejection of
monarchical authority in the revolutions of the eighteenth and
nineteenth centuries.[2] To some extent, then, the paradigm of
authority we have discussed above was in response to the
Protestant position as much as to the disorder of the revolution, (in Latourette's sense).

The second major theological current against which the
theology of the magisterium of the Roman School was still reacting and which influenced the formation of the paradigm was
Gallicanism. Congar reminds us that "in the great debate that
dominated ecclesiological theory from the eleventh to the nineteenth century in the West, which can be characterized as a ten-
sion between two poles, 'pontifical monarchy' and 'Church,'
Gallicanism gave the importance to the Church. . . ."[3] In an
era concerned so much with authority, it is not surprising that
this theory should continue to be seen as a threat. The continuing tendency of the French bishops to assert their national-
ism was a threat to papal authority even in the reign of Pius XI
(in the case of L'Action Française).

Last but not least of the theological movements that were
influential in the development of the paradigms was that of
Modernism. We have seen that Billot's De Immutabilitate

---

[1]Bellamy, La Théologie Catholique au XIXe Siecle, p. 227;
Congar, Lay People in the Church, pp. 45 and passim.

[2]Congar, "Le Peuple Fidèle et la Fonction Prophetique de
l'Eglise," p. 79.

[3]Congar, Lay People in the Church, p. 41. He points out
here the various phases of Gallicanism and its several possible
meanings.

Traditionis was specifically directed against Loisy. If anything suppressed the possible emergence of new paradigms of
truth in the first half of the twentieth century, it was the
strong reaction of Rome to Modernism. We will discuss this in
greater detail in the following chapter, but the point to be
made here is that the essentialist, a-historical paradigm of
truth reasserted by Billot was in response to Modernism.

By way of summary of this point, speaking not only of the
doctrine of the magisterium in the Roman School but of the whole
De Ecclesia tract, Congar says:

> The treatise on the Church is a particular treatise com-
> posed in answer to Gallicanism, to conciliarism, to the
> purely spiritual ecclesiology of Wycliff and Hus, to
> Protestant negations, later on to those of secular
> 'stateism,' Modernism and so on. It follows that it is
> composed in reaction against errors all of which call the
> hierarchical structure of the Church in question. The de
> Ecclesia was principally, sometimes almost exclusively,
> a defence and affirmation of the reality of the Church as
> machinery of hierarchical mediation, of the powers and
> primacy of the Roman See, in a word, a 'hierarchology.'[1]

Neither these theological currents, nor the general cultural context of Western Europe can give a full explanation of
how or why the paradigms of truth, of authority, or of the socio-
political structure of the church which we have seen in the
theology of the magisterium, have emerged. Our brief remarks
suffice to show that such paradigms were not entirely divorced
from the cultural context, nor were they deliberately and consciously chosen by the individual theologians. They were the
shared presuppositions of the community of practitioners, their
"disciplinary matrix." It was not our intention, however, to
explain their origin or relation to the society; but merely to
describe them. It should be clear now that there were such paradigms operative in the theology of the magisterium of the Roman
School. What happens to these paradigms when the awareness of

---

[1]Congar, Lay People in the Church, p. 45.

anomaly spreads through the discipline, we will see in the next chapter.

CHAPTER V

PARADIGMS IN TRANSITION

Having described the teaching of the Roman School on the
doctrine of the magisterium up to the time of Vatican II, and
having examined the paradigms that were operative in that teaching, I wish now to indicate that these paradigms are no longer
the dominant ones in the Roman Catholic theological community
and that the current disagreement (or crisis) may be understood
as the process of shifting from that set of paradigms to a new
set, not yet established but seeking the adherence of the community of practitioners. I will indicate the various phases of
this process of shifting according to Kuhn's theory (not necessarily in temporal sequence) and show how they are verifiable in
the current situation. It is worth noting once again, I believe,
that Kuhn's theory is being employed only analogously. I will
try to point out similarities and dissimilarities as we proceed.
In the final section, I will suggest some of the alternate
paradigms that are currently competing for the allegiance of the
Roman Catholic theological community.

Kuhn's Theory of Shifting Paradigms

Discovery or "novelty of fact" as well as invention or
"novelty of theory" commences with the awareness of anomaly,
according to Kuhn. Anomaly means the violation of the "paradigm-
induced expectations that govern normal science."[1] In any
developed science, there are some paradigms operative at all
times. It is against the horizon of the dominant paradigms that
anomaly appears. Kuhn says that "research under a paradigm must

---

[1]Kuhn, The Structure of Scientific Revolutions, pp. 52-53.

be a particularly effective way of inducing paradigm change."[1]

Some anomaly occurs by accident as in the case of X-rays, but
more often novelty of fact is the result of ever-more refined
instrumentation and observation suggested by the paradigm then
in possession. In the process of pursuing "normal science"
("extending the knowledge of those facts that the paradigm displays as particularly revealing, by increasing the extent of
the match between those facts and the paradigm's predictions,
and by further articulation of the paradigm itself")[2] that
anomalies of fact are recognized. For our purposes in theology,
it is important to stress this function of the older paradigm in
giving birth to a new one. The new paradigm may, and usually
does, require the repudiation of the older one, but this does
not necessarily imply that the older one had no value, or even
that it was not "true" in some sense. Because of the parallel
to our own recent situation in theology on this point, it is
worth quoting Kuhn at some length:

> Further development, therefore, ordinarily calls for the
> construction of elaborate equipment, the development of an
> esoteric vocabulary and skills, and a refinement of concepts
> that increasingly lessens their resemblance to their usual
> common-sense prototypes. That professionalization leads, on
> the one hand, to an immense restriction of the scientist's
> vision and to a considerable resistance to paradigm change.
> The science has become increasingly rigid. On the other
> hand, within those areas to which the paradigm directs the
> attention of the group, normal science leads to a detail of
> information and to a precision of the observation-theory
> match that could be achieved in no other way. Furthermore,
> that detail and precision-of-match have a value that trans-
> cends their not always very high intrinsic interest. With-
> out the special apparatus that is constructed mainly for
> anticipated functions, the results that lead ultimately to
> novelty could not occur. And even when the apparatus exists,
> novelty ordinarily emerges only for the man who, knowing
> with precision what he should expect, is able to recognize
> that something has gone wrong. Anomaly appears only against
> the background provided by the paradigm.[3]

---

[1]Ibid. [2]Ibid., p. 24.

[3]Kuhn, The Structure of Scientific Revolutions, pp. 64-65.

Except for the references to "equipment" and "apparatus," most of the other characteristics of the development of "normal science" can be found in the Roman School of theology we have examined in Chapters II and III. These characteristics are true of all the so-called "manual theologies" of which the Roman School is a paradigmatic example. "The development of an esoteric vocabulary," "the refinement of concepts that increasingly lessens their resemblance to their usual common-sense prototypes," "the restriction of the scientist's (read theologian) vision," and a "considerable resistance to paradigm change," are all verified in the case of the doctrine of the magisterium of the Roman School. Without repeating all that we have already said, recall, for example, the preoccupation with and the terminology of the on-going discussion concerning the relation of the potestas ordinis, potestas jurisdictionis and potestas docendi. The vocabulary is certainly esoteric, the concepts refined, and the theologians vision restricted in that case. Yet unless these questions had been pursued to the point of losing their resemblance to common-sense experience, the awareness of anomaly would not have come about. This background-function of one paradigm, or set of paradigms, for the emergence of another set is the thread of continuity in the discipline. "Novelty of theory," with which theology is more concerned, is even more dependent on awareness of anomaly than is "novelty of fact."[1] The kind of theory that Kuhn is talking about is such as the Copernican versus Ptolemaic astronomic theory. This involves a paradigm shift on a far wider scale than is required for discovery or "novelty of fact." It is not just an isolated phenomenon that must be seen in a totally different way, but a

---

[1]Kuhn, The Structure of Scientific Revolutions, p. 67. Although Kuhn makes this distinction, he says it is "exceedingly artificial" (p. 52), and the two are so closely related that the distinction ceases to be significant.

132

very fundamental view of the universe. A theory organizes a
whole wide range of data and has more far-reaching consequences.
Hence, a paradigm shift on the level of theory is both rarer and
more revolutionary. Kuhn says, "Because it demands large-scale
paradigm destruction and major shifts in the problems and
techniques of normal science, the emergence of new theories is
generally preceded by a period of pronounced professional
insecurity."[1]

Although there are "novelties of fact" in theology, in the
sense of new historical or archeological data, the kind of
paradigm shift that I am suggesting as pertinent to the doctrine
of the magisterium is more akin to that of theory than that of
fact. The paradigms that are operative in that doctrine--of
authority, of truth, of teaching, of the socio-political structure of the church--are on the level of theory rather than that
of fact. More exactly, they are conceptual paradigms although,
like most concepts, have some concrete image underlying them--
think of the pyramid model of authority, or the "deposit" model
of truth that we have indicated was operative for the Roman
School. Changes in paradigms on this level, then, will be of
far broader consequence and far more unsettling than changes of
paradigms occasioned by novelty of fact. Both however, begin
with the awareness and recognition of anomaly.

Perhaps we should recall here the underlying assumption of
this study which was stated briefly in the Preface. The relation
between fact and theory, between "knowledge and its social base
is a dialectical one, that is, knowledge is a social product and
knowledge is a factor in social change."[2] While this thesis is
concerned only with the level of knowledge, of theory, of

_____

[1]Ibid., pp. 67-68.

[2]Berger and Luckmann, The Social Construction of Reality,
p. 87.

theology, we are acutely aware that the lived experience of the Roman Catholic community as a whole (not just that of the theologians) is a factor in the awareness of anomaly on the part of the theologians. Large segments of the Roman Catholic populace seem to have decided that the magisterial authority is being misused, or at least exceeding its proper limits and functions. The response has been at times rebellion, at times to ignore the magisterial statements, and at other times, to suffer severe anguish of conscience. Whatever the reaction, this experience of the people as a whole has been a factor in the crisis on the level of theory. It is a fact (however difficult to prove empirically) and has been an important element in the crisis of the magisterium.[1]

After the awareness and recognition of an anomalous situation, there is usually a concentration of research in the area of anomaly. If the anomaly persists over a period of time, or if there are other circumstances, either internal or external to the discipline, which make the anomaly particularly pressing, then the anomaly "comes to seem more than just another puzzle of normal science, (and) the transition to crisis and to extraordinary science has begun."[2] The anomaly may be recognized at first by only a restricted segment of the community of practitioners but as it develops into a crisis more and more of the eminent men in the discipline become concerned with the problem

---

[1]There is need for sociological and psychological research on how and why the attitudes of the Roman Catholic populace have shifted so dramatically and suddenly, apparently since the 1950's. The only study with which I am familiar is the one recently commissioned by and presented to the American Catholic bishops on the attitudes of priests. This study was carried out by the National Opinion Research Center at the University of Chicago but has not yet been made public. Lacking such research, it is difficult to discuss with any validity the social reality which is the basis of the emerging theology.

[2]Kuhn, The Structure of Scientific Revolutions, p. 82.

134

area. It is then that the period of "professional insecurity",
mentioned above, occurs.

The increased interest and research in the area of anomaly
leads to suggested modifications of the theory or paradigm on
which the discipline has been operating. Kuhn says that
"proliferation of versions of a theory is a very usual symptom
of crisis."[1] The previous paradigms and rules of operation in
"normal science" become blurred and few of the practitioners can
agree on what the rules or the paradigms are. There is an
uncomfortable state of confusion in the discipline. New theories
are then put forward in attempts to deal with the anomaly more
successfully.

The gradual move into "extraordinary science," that is,
a state of crisis, is usually accompanied by a turn to philosophical analysis on the part of scientists--a procedure they
normally eschew. But they are now more inclined to examine the
presuppositions of their discipline and questions of methodology
loom larger in their minds.

Kuhn summarizes the characteristics of a discipline moving
from a period of normalcy to one of crisis as follows: "The
proliferation of competing articulations, the willingness to try
anything, the expression of explicit discontent, the recourse to
philosophy and to debate over fundamentals, all these are
symptoms of a transition from normal to extraordinary research."[2]
It begins with a "sense of malfunction" that can lead to crisis
and finally to a "revolution" or shift in paradigms.

Kuhn defines scientific revolutions as "those non-cumula-
tive developmental episodes in which an older paradigm is

[1]Ibid., p. 71.

[2]Kuhn, The Structure of Scientific Revolutions, p. 91.

replaced in whole or in part by an incompatible new one."[1] This
is really a paradigm-shift, but he feels the word "revolution"
is justifiable in terms of the parallel he finds to political
revolutions, and this in two respects: First of all,

> Political revolutions are inaugurated by a growing sense,
> often restricted to a segment of the political community,
> that existing institutions have ceased adequately to meet
> the problems posed by an environment that they have in part
> created. In much the same way, scientific revolutions are
> inaugurated by a growing sense, again often restricted to a
> narrow subdivision of the scientific community, that an
> existing paradigm has ceased to function adequately in the
> exploration of an aspect of nature to which that paradigm
> itself had previously led the way. In both political and
> scientific development the sense of malfunction that can
> lead to crisis is prerequisite to revolution.[2]

This is the genetic or developmental aspect of the parallel, but

there is another and, Kuhn says, more profound aspect of

similarity. I would like to quote him again at some length

because it also applies in a most striking way to the changes

taking place in the theology of the magisterium and in the

institutional life of the church as I will try to show in the

rest of this chapter. The second aspect of similarity is in the

manner of choice among competing paradigms. Kuhn says:

> Political revolutions aim to change political institutions
> in ways that those institutions themselves prohibit. Their
> success therefore necessitates the partial relinquishment
> of one set of institutions in favor of another, and in the
> interim, society is not fully governed by institutions at
> all. Initially it is crisis alone that attenuates the role
> of political institutions as we have already seen it atten-
> uate the role of paradigms. In increasing numbers individuals
> become increasingly estranged from political life and behave
> more and more eccentrically within it. Then, as the crisis
> deepens, many of these individuals commit themselves to some
> concrete proposal for the reconstruction of society in a new
> institutional framework. At that point the society is
> divided into competing camps or parties, one seeking to
> defend the old institutional constellation, the others
> seeking to institute some new one.[3]

---

[1]Ibid., p. 92.

[2]Kuhn, The Structure of Scientific Revolutions, p. 92.

[3]Ibid., p. 93.

At this point, Kuhn remarks, that "political recourse fails," and the choice is like that between competing paradigms--it is a choice between "incompatible modes of community life." The issue is not something that can be settled by logic or experiment alone. "Each group uses its own paradigm to argue in that paradigm's defense." The argumentation becomes circular and it cannot compel those who refuse to step into the circle. Ultimately, "As in political revolutions, so in paradigm choice --there is no standard higher than the assent of the relevant community."[1]

It is on this point that Kuhn has been accused of being too subjectivistic and of making the scientific enterprise an a-rational one.[2] But that criticism seems deliberately to misunderstand his point, which is that a paradigm change is a basically different way of "seeing" the world, that it involves not only facts but values and presuppositions. A change on a level as fundamental as this (again he recalls the analogy of the gestalt switch) is more a matter of persuasion and conversion than of merely logical argumentation. That, however, does not make it irrational nor a matter of some "mystical" experience. Kuhn summarizes his own refutation of his critics on this point as follows:

> The conversion experience that I have likened to a gestalt switch remains, therefore, at the heart of the revolutionary process. Good reasons for choice provide motives for conversion and a climate in which it is more

---

[1] Kuhn, The Structure of Scientific Revolutions, p. 94.

[2] See Dudley Shapere, "Meaning and Scientific Change," in Mind and Cosmos: Essays in Contemporary Science and Philosophy, The University of Pittsburgh Series in the Philosophy of Science III (Pittsburgh: The University Press, 1966), 41-85; and by the same author, his review, "The Structure of Scientific Revolutions" The Philosophical Review, LXXII, (1964), 383-94; Karl R. Popper, "Normal Science and its Dangers," and Imre Lakatos, "Falsification and the Methodology of Scientific Research Programmes," both in Criticism and the Growth of Knowledge, Imre Lakatos and Alan Musgrave, eds. (Cambridge: The University Press, 1970).

likely to occur. Translation may, in addition, provide
points of entry for the neural reprogramming that, however
inscrutable at this time, must underlie conversion. But
neither good reasons nor translation constitute conversion,
and it is that process we must explicate in order to understand an essential sort of scientific change.[1]

Theologians should have less difficulty understanding this point

than Kuhn's scientific or philosophical critics (e.g., Lonergan's

notion of "conversion").

Since it is a process of persuasion, language becomes a

critical problem and hence, the reference to "translation" in

the citation above. There is a problem of communication--"Two

men who perceive the same situation differently but nevertheless

employ the same vocabulary in its discussion must be using words

differently. They speak, that is, from what I have called

incommensurable viewpoints. How can they even hope to talk

together much less to be persuasive."[2] After some discussion

of the process of sensation and response to stimuli, he says

that those who experience such communication breakdowns can at

least "recognize each other as members of different language

communities and then become translators." They can at least

refrain from explaining the others' behavior as error or madness.

In theology, this could mean that charges of heterodoxy would

be rarer occurrences.

The choice between competing paradigms cannot be decided

by the criteria of "normal science" because that always pre-

supposes some paradigm, and each paradigm justifies itself on

the basis of its own criteria. It is a question of values that

"can be answered only in terms of criteria that lie outside of

normal science altogether, and it is that recourse to external

---

[1] Kuhn, The Structure of Scientific Revolutions, p. 204.

[2] Ibid., p. 200.

criteria that most obviously makes paradigm debates revolutionary."[1] The competing paradigms are compared and tested--compared with one another and with nature--but the choice is not made on that basis alone. The criteria external to the discipline itself play a significant role.

Not only are there external criteria involved in the choice of paradigms, but there are external factors active in precipitating the crisis. Kuhn gives the example of the social pressure for calendar reform, the medieval criticism of Aristotle and the rise of Renaissance Neoplatonism as factors in the Copernican revolution. "In a mature science . . . external factors like those cited above are principally significant in determining the timing of breakdown, the ease with which it can be recognized, and the area in which, because it is given particular attention, the breakdown first occurs."[2] Such factors external to theology itself, are also operative in the present crisis.

It is important to note that one of the external factors that differs significantly in the case of the breakdown of theological paradigms is the structure of the community itself. Although we have spoken of theologians as a "community of practitioners" which they are, and to this extent the theological community is parallel to the scientific community, the former is only part of a larger community to which they are in service. Theologians exist as part of a much more structured community, with authorities over and above the theologians themselves and with beliefs shared by a much wider community than that of the professional theologians. The authorities in a scientific community are the scientists themselves, and the beliefs of the

[1]Kuhn, The Structure of the Scientific Revolutions, p. 110.

[2]Ibid., p. 69.

scientific community are determined by the scientists, not by a broader population, nor by antiquity, nor by external authorities. The practitioners of a scientific discipline are autonomous; theologians are not.

The two issues mentioned at the beginning of this study as focusing the crisis in the magisterium today (birth control and celibacy of the clergy) are factors external to the theology of the magisterium itself. They are, however, very much part of the life of the Christian community, and since theologians are part of that wider community, such factors cannot be said to be external in the same way that they would be for a scientific community. The experience of the Christian community is data for the theologian, whereas data for the scientific community in the sciences from which Kuhn takes his examples is confined to more controlable experiential evidence, and social experiences and pressures are easily said to be "external."

In concluding this description of the process of paradigm change according to Kuhn, we shall cite two conditions which he argues must be met by a paradigm seeking the allegiance of the community: "First, the new candidate must seem to resolve some outstanding and generally recognized problem that can be met in no other way. Second, the new paradigm must promise to preserve a relatively large part of the concrete problem-solving ability that has accrued to science through its predecessors."[1] In other words, despite all the external factors involved, the new paradigm must respond to the felt needs of the community of practitioners without overturning all the past achievements of that community. It may require adjustment of some of the acquired knowledge in the discipline and it may be seen in a totally new light, but it does not reject all the achievements

---

[1]Kuhn, The Structure of Scientific Revolutions, p. 169.

140

of the past. Despite connotations to the contrary, no revolution ever does totally reject the past.

Lastly, before applying this theory to the current crisis
of the magisterium, it is well to recall again that the process
of shifting paradigms is one that takes time--sixty to a
hundred years in a natural science and perhaps longer in the
case of a less exact discipline--and it may be resolved only
with the death of the adherents of the older paradigm. "The
transfer of allegiance from paradigm to paradigm is a conversion
experience that cannot be forced."[1] Even if we understand the
process, the outcome cannot be induced by coercion. To realize
this may help us to live with the crisis a bit better.

Paradigm Shifts in the Theology of the Magisterium

Without seeming to force Kuhn's categories on the theological situation, there are a number of factors in the theology
of the magisterium which seem accurately described in the theory
just outlined. This is, admittedly, an interpretation, but
with sufficient basis in fact to be justified. What is the
source of anomaly in the Roman Catholic theological world that
has given rise to a sense of "crisis"? I would suggest two
factors. First, and this has been with us much longer and is
more acutely and more widely felt now, is the historical awareness, the sense of history, of the relativities of history--it
can be described in many ways--perhaps it is most adequately
stated by Langdon Gilkey when he says:

> Where are the ultimate events of revelation when all in
> history swims in the relativity of time; what is the Word
> of God amidst the welter and variety of historical words
> in scripture; what is the mind of the Church in the mani-
> fold of changing historical minds, each rooted in and so
> directly relevant only to its own epoch? The divine bases

[1]Ibid., p. 151.

> for authority in theology seem to have fled with this
> historicizing of everything historical, leaving us with
> only the tatters of merely human authorities . . . [1]

This is a twentiety-century non-Roman Catholic speaking and
accurately states the problem as it occurs today, but it is not
exactly the way it would have been posed when it first arose.
The threat was not seen as one directly affecting authority as
much as it was a threat to the truth and certainty of revealed
doctrine. The expectations induced by the paradigms of the
Roman School were not fulfilled by the growth of historical
studies in the nineteenth century. The notion that truth was
one and immutable did not prepare them for the varieties of
opinion and even of doctrine discovered in the Fathers and in
the history of the church. It seemed that historical fact did
not always support the idea that what is now held and taught by
the church was always held and taught by the church.

When it came to the specific doctrine of the magisterium,
we have seen how the Roman School labored to deal with the
"counterinstances" of Liberius, Honorius and with councils that
did not seem to support their position.[2] Such instances had to
be justified on the basis of theory or interpretation, and
Billot could state as a principle that if the Fathers could be
interpreted in an "orthodox" way, they should be.[3] The other
principle that if the church defined something at one period in
her history, she must always have taught it, was a similar
attempt to deal with the uncertainties of historical research.

The growth of historical awareness gave rise to a sense
of anomaly among theologians besides those of the Roman School
and, indeed, more severely elsewhere. The interest in historical studies at Tübingen, which culminated in Döllinger's

---

[1] Langdon Gilkey, *Naming the Whilwind: The Renewal of God-
Language* (New York: Bobbs-Merrill Company, 1969), p. 51.

[2] E.g., Mazzella, pp. 866 ff.   [3] *Supra*, Chapter III.

refusal to accept the decree of Vatican I, was one instance.
The efforts of Newman and the Modernists to deal with this problem are more significant because much of what they said then
has come to be acceptable today, and I will treat them at some
length shortly. The overall reaction of Roman Catholic theology
to the problems raised by the new historical consciousness was
a negative one--a retreat to a non-historical approach, a
renewal of scholasticism,[1] and a fear of the consequences of a
recognition of the "facts." The latter half of the nineteenth
century and the early part of the twentiety century saw little
real progress in dealing with the problem. Shoof accurately
describes the period when he says:

> In the first place, the creative theological impulse, which
> was, in the context of the whole Church, still very weak,
> went dead to a great extent and its place was soon taken by
> a new theological attitude. On the one hand, Catholic
> theologians together with the whole Church, took up a
> resolutely defensive position. In opposition to the new
> thinking that was so concerned with empirical facts, a
> theology was developed which Welte has strikingly described
> as a 'theology despite everything' and a 'safeguarding of
> orthodoxy that was not without a certain nervousness.' On
> the other hand, scholastic thought, which was dormant in the
> Church, discovered that it was spiritually remarkably close
> to the new objective and analytical thought in the world.
> Scholastic thought is also analytical and deals in an objec-
> tive and apparently mathematical way with an ever increasing
> number of more and more precisely defined concepts, thus
> integrating the reality of salvation--into separate atoms.
> The direct consequence of these two theologiclal tenden-
> cies--the defensive attitude of theology and the interest
> in scholasticism--was the sudden revival of scholastic
> thought in a form that was more apologetical and even more
> polemical than before, namely neo-scholasticism.[2]

This, however, was only to delay the crisis, not to solve it.
The two world wars in Europe postponed its resolution even
longer. Hence, it is understandable that, though the awareness

---

[1]It must be noted, however, that in the more recent part
of our period there are theologians in the neo-scholastic tradition who are quite historically conscious, such as Yves Congar,
Karl Rahner, Bernard Lonergan and M.D. Chenu.

[2]T. M. Shoof, A Survey of Catholic Theology: 1800-1970,
trans. by N.D. Smith (Glen Rock, N.J.: Paulist Newman Press,
1970), pp. 33-36.

of anomaly based on the growth of historical consciousness has
been with us a long time, the actual period of crisis was able
to arise only in our own time.

The second factor which may be described as anomalous is
that of pluralism. This is somewhat later in its impact on
theology and only in the decades immediately preceding Vatican
II was it dealt with explicitly. The ecumenical movement
may be described as a response to it, but this movement has had
many phases itself. By pluralism I mean, in the ecclesiological
context, the fact that there seems to be more than one institutional means by which God intends the salvation of all men. It
amounts to a radical revision (if not denial) of the old adage
that "There is no salvation outside the church." The uniqueness
and exclusivity of the Roman Catholic church as a visible
institution is seriously questioned.

The source of both of these factors of anomaly is the
experience of the contemporary Christian. He is unwilling to
accept the assertion that his friends and neighbors, whom he
knows to be "good people," are condemned to eternal damnation
because they are "heretics," "schismatics," or just plain
"pagans." Nor is he willing to accept the assumption that what
is has always been the teaching of the church, when he is so
aware of the cultural and historical relativities of his own
time. A theology which does not account for these variables of
his own experience, cannot be true. It cannot be true because
it is not true to his experience. That experience should enter
in as a criterion of truth in theology is surely a novelty in
comparison with the Roman School. In any case, it is the source
of the anomaly that has developed into a full-scale crisis in
the Roman Catholic church. How these two factors of anomaly
have been dealt with in Roman Catholic theology we will discuss

briefly a little later. Before we do that, however, it would
seem appropriate to indicate the other similarities to Kuhn's
theory of paradigm-change that appear in the theological scene.

The recognition of anomaly, according to Kuhn, is usually
followed by a concentration of research in the area of anomaly.
Broadly speaking, the "return to the sources" movement in
Catholic theology in the past ninety years or so is a manifestation of this phenomenon. The renewed interest in patristics,
in biblical studies, and in the history of theology was an
exploration of the area of anomaly--the historical consciousness. That interest had begun in the first half of the nineteenth century in such places as Rome (Perrone, Passaglia and
Schrader) and Tübingen (Drey, Sailer and Möhler), and it is this
tendency to which Shoof refers as the "creative theological
impulse" (cf. page 152). Shoof describes in more general terms
the development I have indicated in the limited sphere of the
theology of the magisterium of the Roman School, namely that
there was a change in the later half of the nineteenth century
to a more juridical and more scholastic approach to theology.
There seems to be no clear-cut explanation for this change in
interest, but undobtedly the political situation in Europe and
the defensive reaction of Pius IX had something to do with it.
In any case, the return to historical studies lost momentum
until the early part of the twentieth century.

Two other characteristics that Kuhn mentions which follow
the recognition of anomaly--its initial restriction to a small
segment of the professional community which later grows gradually to concern more and more men in the discipline with the
area of anomaly, and, secondly, that a period of "professional
insecurity" is likely--both are obvious, I should think, to one
familiar with the recent history of Roman Catholic theology.

The increased preoccupation with the question of "development of
doctrine" in the latter part of the period, had bothered only
Newman, the Modernists and few others in the early half of the
period. The period of "professional insecurity" is an accurate
if somewhat euphemistic description of the atmosphere created
by the fusillade of condemnations issuing from the Vatican since
the time of Pius IX.[1] Most theological innovations or creative
impulses were stifled or driven underground right up until
Vatican II. Only recently has the insecurity focused on the
magisterium itself and on authority in the church.

The characteristic recourse to philosophy and to debate
over fundamentals has also been occuring recently in Roman
Catholic theology as evidenced by the growing concern with
methodology. The place and function of the magisterium is very
much bound up with the question of theological methodology con-
sidering the strong position magisterial statements have
occupied in recent Roman Catholic theology. This study itself
reflects that concern.

Perhaps the most striking parallel in the theology of the
magisterium to Kuhn's theory of paradigm-change is the proliferation of theories or of versions of a theory which follows
the awareness of anomaly and is "a very usual symptom of crisis."[2]
I will select only a few of the most important attempts and try
to indicate the paradigms presupposed therein. This will serve,
I hope, to clarify by contrast the paradigms operative in the
Roman School already described.

---

[1]E.G., Syllabus of Errors, 1864, the anathemas of Vatican
I, 1870, Post obitum, 1887, Providentissimus Deus, 1893, Testem
benevolentiae, 1899, Lamentabili, 1907, Pascendi dominici gregis,
1907, Quam singulari, 1910, Sacrorum antistites (Oath against
Modernism), 1910, Divini illius magistri, 1929, Casti connubii,
1930, and numerous responses of the Biblical Commission.

[2]Supra, pp. 143-144.

146

Some Early Attempts--Newman and the Modernists

Without trying to survey the recent history of Catholic
ecclesiology, I want merely to indicate that there have been
some attempts to deal with the two sources of anomaly--historical
consciousness and pluralism--previous to the contemporary crisis.
Newman and the Modernists (as represented by Tyrrell and Loisy)
have been selected both because of their significance then and
the fact that they became even more influential later in our
period. This is not intended to be a paradigm analysis of the
teaching of these men, but only an indication of how they
differed from the theology of the magisterium of the Roman
School and what paradigms were different from those we have seen
in the Gregorian professors. The treatment will necessarily be
brief and incomplete, but Newman and the Modernists are not the
object of this study; they are background characters in the
cast.[1]

Newman was not deliberately trying to suggest alternate
paradigms to those of the Roman School. His thought is personal and independent of the main currents of Roman Catholic
thought of his time. He was, however, trying to come to terms
with the facts of history while maintaining the doctrinal
principle. This sets him off from the dominant Roman Catholic
theology of the time. Referring to his essay, "On Consulting
the Faithful," Baum says:

> This essay brought to a head the conflict between the
> historical mentality of Newman and the dogmatic approach
> of the Catholic establishment. Newman's adversaries
> regarded the conclusion of the essay to be contrary to
> defined Catholic teaching. Since the Church was
> irrevocably gifted with an infallible magisterium, her
> history ought always to be understood in terms of these
> underlying principles. The historical approach, Newman's

---

[1]For fuller studies on Newman and the Modernists, consult
the bibliography.

adversaries felt, led to confusion among the people,
endangered the revealed faith, and promoted a purely
human approach to the sacred reality of the Church.[1]

Newman's adversaries were not primarily the Roman theologians, although Passaglia lectured against his position without
naming him specifically.[2] Newman found Perrone more to his
liking and presented him with a series of theses in which he
tried to set forth his theory of development in formal theological language.[3] As Chadwick points out, "the document adds
little or nothing to our knowledge of Newman's thought in 1845-
47, being a summary of the main ideas of the Essay, a summary
which is sometimes less cloudy than the original . . ." and
"Perrone laconically but flatly denied Newman's thesis."[4] With
regard to the magisterium, Newman thought that the mind of the
church has to be discovered by "meditation, discussion, dialec-
tic" before a definition can be achieved, whereas Perrone thought
that definition was merely a seal of truth on a matter that had
always been clear in the mind of the church.[5] When Newman raised
the question of various historical instances which the old
theory could not explain--the validity of heretical baptism, the
canon of scripture, the sinlessness of the Virgin Mary, the
doctrine of indulgences, etc.--Perrone merely wrote, Haec omnia

[1]Gregory Baum, in the "Foreward" to Samuel D. Femiano,
Infallibility of the Laity (New York: Herder & Herder, 1967),
pp. x-xi.

[2]Chadwick, From Bossuet to Newman, p. 174. Chief among his
attackers were the conservative English professor of theology at
Ushaw, Dr.Gillow, and the American polemecist, himself recently
converted to Roman Catholicism, Orestes Brownson.

[3]Cf. T. Lynch, ed., "The Newman-Perrone Paper on Development," previously cited.

[4]Chadwick, From Bossuet to Newman, p. 182, referring primarily to Newman's analogy between the faith of an individual
and the corporate faith of the church.

[5]Chadwick, From Bossuet to Newman, pp. 182-83.

148

semper tenuit Ecclesia ac professa est.[1]

Newman discussed the matter of the consensus fidelium with
Perrone and felt, especially after the publication of the
latter's De immaculato B. V. Mariae conceptu (1852) that they
did not basically disagree. Indeed, he cites Perrone's work at
some length in his Rambler article, "On Consulting the Faithful,"
to this effect.[2] But Newman's interest in the function of the
faithful in doctrinal decisions was based on historical facts
and the necessity to take account of them. That was the point
of the long discussion of the Arian controversy at the end of the
Rambler article. Perrone's position was founded in a concern to
explain a present dogmatic position for which concrete historical evidence was lacking. It would appear that Perrone did not
see Newman's problem at all.[3]

Though Newman and Perrone had, I believe, some fundamental
disagreements, Newman's understanding of the nature and function
of the magisterium did not differ much from that of the Roman
School. He placed as much emphasis on authority as did the
Roman theologians; indeed, for Newman, "The essence of all
religion is authority and obedience."[4] This was especially necessary at his time he felt, but it was also necessary if there
had been revelation given. He says:

> The absolute need of a spiritual supremacy is at present
> the strongest of arguments in favour of the fact of its
> supply. Surely, either an objective revelation has not
> been given, or it has been provided with means for impres-
> sing its objectiveness on the world. If Christianity be a

---

[1]T. Lynch, "The Newman-Perrone Paper on Development,"
pp. 428-29.

[2]John Henry Newman, On Consulting the Faithful in Matters
of Doctrine, edited and with an introduction by John Coulson
(London: Geoffrey Chapman, 1961), pp. 64 ff.

[3]Chadwick, From Bossuet to Newman, p. 183.

[4]John Henry Newman, An Essay on the Development of
Christian Doctrine (Garden City, N.Y.: Doubleday & Company, Inc.
1960), p. 103.

social religion, as it certainly is, and if it be based on certain ideas acknowledge as divine, or a creed (which shall here be assumed), and if these ideas have various aspects, and make distinct impressions on different minds, and issue in consequence in a multiplicity of developments true, or false, or mixed, as has been shown, what power will suffice to meet and to do justice to these conflicting conditions but a supreme authority ruling and reconciling individual judgments by a divine right and a recognized wisdom?[1]

This argument that an infallible teaching authority was the most suitable means for preserving and propagating the revelation was typical of the Roman School, as we have seen.[2]

The function of this magisterium is to "define and declare doctrine," and by this activity the subjective word of God becomes objective, or dogma.[3] He lays more emphasis on the function of the laity as an organ of tradition in enabling the magisterium to come to such definitions and declarations than did the Roman School and stresses that the supreme authority does not act in isolation from the Orbis terrarum when it does give decisions.[4] It was this stress on the necessity of "consulting" the faithful that caused such a stir over the Rambler article.[5] But when it comes to the subject who exercises the authoritative teaching office and the object about which this authority may be exercised, Newman does not differ from the position of the Gregorian professors already outlined.

In what sense then, can Newman be said to be dealing with the sources of anomaly and providing alternate paradigms to the

---

[1]Ibid., p. 106.   [2]Supra., Chs. II and III.

[3]T. Lynch, "The Newman-Perrone Paper on Development," pp. 406-07, and the discussion of this in Femiano, Infallibility of the Laity, pp. 42 ff.; J. -H. Walgrave, Newman the Theologian, trans. by A. V. Littledale (New York: Sheed & Ward, 1960), p. 53.

[4]Günter Biemer, Newman on Tradition, trans. and edited by Kevin Smyth (New York: Herder & Herder, 1967), pp. 106-07.

[5]Newman, On Consulting the Faithful, pp. 54 ff.

ones operative in the Roman School? Of the four paradigms which
I have suggested are operative in the doctrine of the magisterium
of the Roman School--that of the socio-political structure of the
church, of authority, of truth (the epistemological paradigm),
and of teaching--Newman would differ only on the last two,
though his version of all four would be less juridical than
those of the Roman School.

Although he speaks of the "deposit of faith," it is not
once and for all given the way it is for the Gregorian professors. "The deposit of faith is not 'a list of articles that can
be numbered,' and it is 'not a number of formulae.' It is
rather 'a divine philosophy . . . a system of thought' . . . 'a
large philosophy, all parts of which are connected together . . .
so that he who really knows one part, may be said to know all,
as ex pede Herculem.'"[1] The truth is given to the church by the
apostles in the concrete form of the creed but it is "not com-
prehended all at once by the recipients" but requires time and
deep thought for its full elucidation.[2] It is something which
takes possession of the mind and heart. It is the "idea of
Christianity" rather than a series of propositional truths. It
must be worked out and discovered by the church. Hence, there
are two characteristics of Newman's paradigm of truth which are
quite different from the one operative in the Roman School--that
it must necessarily change in order to remain the same,[3] and
that it is a more personal form of knowledge, involving the
heart as well as the head. As Biemer points out, revelation is
the personal self-disclosure of God which demands a personal
response. "The supernatural atmosphere of the traditional

[1]Biemer, Newman on Tradition, pp. 59-60.

[2]Newman, Essay on Development, p. 53.

[3]Ibid., p. 63; Biemer, Newman on Tradition, p. 52;
Walgrave, Newman the Theologian, p. 95.

doctrine, its true 'idea,' its authentic image, must have pene-
trated him (the Christian) and pervade his mind and his heart.
This is the only way in which he can be said to have grasped and
'caught' it, this is the only way of mastering the tradition.
'For surely those only can preach the truth duly who feel it
personally: those only can transmit it fully from God to man,
who have in the transmission made it their own.'"[1] Newman uses
the word "heart" to describe his concept of the personal element
in his model of truth. Thus, it is much different from the
objective conformity between object and intellect which is
immutable and perennially available. It is not a once-and-for-
all given.

Newman's paradigm of teaching-learning is not as
juridical as that of the Roman School for whom it was basically
an exercise of jurisdiction, and it is colored by his notion of
the "illative sense" or the phronema, the instinct or intuition
"deep in the bosom of the mystical body of Christ,"[2] that function of the spirit which perceives truths beyond those furnished
by formal reasoning. The ecclesia docens and the ecclesia
dicens are not as separate or separable as the traditional image
of pastors and sheep would suggest. When it comes to discovering
the mind of the church, all are both teachers and learners. The
function of the official magisterium, is therefore, somewhat
more limited for Newman than for the Roman School, limited to
the function of defining and judging. The entire church,
including the laity, has responsibility for witnessing and
teaching (in non-authoritative ways). Even when it comes to a
definition, there is a conspiratio of the two; "the Church
teaching and the Church taught, are put together, as one twofold

[1]Biemer, Newman on Tradition, pp. 115-16.

[2]Newman, On Consulting the Faithful, p. 73; Biemer,
Newman on Tradition, pp. 61 ff.; Walgrave, Newman on Theologian,
p. 80.

testimony, illustrating each other, and never to be divided.[1]

However much Newman's view of the magisterium may seem in accord with that of the dominant theology of the time, therefore I think it is clear that the paradigms operative in it were somewhat different when it comes to those of truth and teaching. That he was attempting to deal with the area of anomaly we have termed "historical consciousness" I believe is clear from the purpose of his works generally and the Essay on Development of Doctrine and the study on the Arians in particular. One further indication of this attempt lies in the distinction he makes while defending his Rambler article of May, 1859, and that is the distinction between the sensus historicus and the sensus dogmaticus. The first refers to the "real situation," the second to the theological principles which govern the dogmatic stance.[2] However much the distinction may seem (as it does to this writer) like a restatement of the problem, it is an attempt to deal with the problems raised by the historico-critical method.

More specifically and directly than Newman the Modernists were concerned with the problems arising from the development of the historico-critical method--problems for the traditional Roman Catholic attitudes toward Scripture and dogma. Although Newman is the only nineteenth century Catholic theologian whom the Modernists found useful,[3] as Vidler points out, he would have been horrified by the positions of Loisy and Tyrrell. Newman had been concerned with the reasons for belief, the

---

[1] Newman, On Consulting the Faithful, p. 71.

[2] Newman, On Consulting the Faithful, p. 113; Femiano, Infallibility of the Laity, p. 127.

[3] Alec R. Vidler, The Modernist Movement in the Roman Church (Cambridge: The University Press, 1934), pp. 51, 59, 94.

psychology of it, the _why_; the Modernists were dissatisfied with the _what_--the content of belief.[1] The Modernists could not take for granted, as Newman did, the idea of an apostolic _depositum fidei_. To cite Vidler again:

> The modernists by their acceptance of biblical criticism were driven, and by their sympathy with an evolutionary philosophy were encouraged, to reinterpret, in one way or another, the conception of a final and infallible _depositum fidei_. Newman's theory of deductive development which began where the New Testament left off gave way to a theory of the evolution of dogma which was based on a reading of the New Testament the necessity of which he is not to be blamed for failing to foresee.[2]

What the Modernists had in common with Newman, then, was not so much theories or paradigms, but the awareness of the anomaly introduced into the dominant Roman Catholic theology by the findings of historical research.

Modernism is, of course, a very complex phenomenon both in its origin and in its various representatives.[3] For our purposes here, it will be sufficient to comment on the positions of its two chief representatives, Alfred Loisy and George Tyrrell. These were generally considered to be the leaders of the "movement" and were the men against whom the encyclical _Pascendi_ (1907) was primarily directed.[4]

Alfred Loisy was trained by Louis Duchesne in historical method at the Institut Catholique in Paris and was encouraged by him to pursue his interest in biblical studies. From this expertise arose his concern for the adaptation of Catholic dogma

---

[1] _Ibid._, pp. 54-55.

[2] Vidler, _The Modernist Movement in the Roman Church_, pp. 57-58.

[3] In addition to the works cited here, see the bibliography.

[4] Vidler, _The Modernist Movement in the Roman Church_, pp. 10, 184; E.E.Y. Hales, _The Catholic Church in the Modern World_ (Garden City, N.J.: Doubleday & Company, Inc., 1960), p. 178.

and ecclesiastical structure to the modern world. His concern
was explicitly the historical character of both the church and
the Gospel.[1] The source of his awareness of this anomaly was
his historical research. The first evidence of this was published in the form of a reply to Adolf von Harnack's Das Wesen
des Christenthums (1900), although it was more than just that.[2]
In the Introduction to the fifth edition, Loisy says:

> . . . the twofold object he had in view was tactfully to
> instruct the Catholic clergy about the real situation of
> the problem of Christian origins, while at the same time
> demonstrating against Protestant criticism that this
> situation was far from making a defence of Catholicism
> impossible--that, on the contrary, the Church could now
> be seen as a necessary and legitimate development of the
> Gospel; and that what was rationally untenable was the
> position of Liberal Protestantism with its supposed essence
> of Christianity which had been rediscovered only in our
> own time, after having been lost for more than eighteen
> centuries.[3]

He did this by arguing that Christianity was not some immutable
essence and that Harnack had reduced a complex and living thing
to his own faith, namely, trust in God as Father.[4] Loisy would
find the essence of Christianity "in the fulness and totality of
its life, which shows movement and variety just because it is
life," and he suggests that the historian should return to the
parable of the mustard seed.[5] For Loisy, change is the natural
condition for preservation and expression of vitality of anything, including the church. In a famous passage, frequently
quoted only in truncated form, Loisy says:

---

[1]Shoof, A Survey of Catholic Theology: 1800-1970, p. 54;
John Ratté, Three Modernists (New York: Sheed & Ward, 1967), p. 7.

[2]Alfred Loisy, The Gospel and the Church, trans., by
Christopher Home (1902 rev. ed.; New York: Charles Scribner's
Sons, 1912).

[3]As cited in Alec R. Vidler, 20th Century Defenders of the
Faith (London: SCM Press, 1965), p. 40.

[4]Loisy, The Gospel and the Church, pp. 14 ff.

[5]Ibid., pp. 16-17.

> Jesus foretold the kingdom, and it was the Church that
> came; she came, enlarging the form of the gospel, which
> it was impossible to preserve as it was, as soon as the
> Passion closed the ministry of Jesus. There is no
> institution on earth or in history whose status and value
> may not be questioned if the principle is established that
> nothing may exist except in its original form. Such a
> principle is contrary to the law of life, which is movement
> and a continual effort of adaptation to conditions always
> new and perpetually changing. Christianity has not escaped
> this law, and cannot be reproached for submission to it.
> It could not do otherwise than it has done.[1]

His contention was that the church (Roman Catholic) had pre-

served "the fundamental idea of Christ's teaching" though it

does not realize the kingdom finally and only prepares the way

for its accomplishment. "If the dimensions of the evangelical

horizon have changed (Christ was mistaken on the imminence of

the eschaton), the point of view remains the same."[2] The

identity of the church, like that of a man, is not determined

by immobile external forms but through the continuity of the

consciousness of life. The church has from the beginning

(including within the Scripture itself) adapted the gospel to the

needs of the men she was addressing.[3] His argument against

Liberal Protestantism and his defence of Roman Catholicism is

that the adaptations and changes that have taken place are not

all distortions and perversions of some primitive essence that

now we can and should recover, but the necessary and legitimate

developments of the gospel, true to Christ's teaching.

It is clear that the fundamental paradigm underlying

Loisy's view of the church, of authority and of magisterial

teaching is an organic and evolutionary one. There is a dis-

tinction between the fundamental ideas of Christ's teaching and

its various historical forms. Speaking of dogmas, he says that,

"The conceptions that the Church presents as revealed dogmas are

---

[1]Loisy, The Gospel and the Church, pp. 166. (Emphasis
mine.)

[2]Ibid., p. 168. [3]Ibid., pp. 170-71, 213.

not truths fallen from heaven, and preserved by religious tradition in the precise form in which they first appeared . . .
Though dogmas may be Divine in origin and substance, they are
human in structure and composition."[1] The ecclesiastical
formula is only an aid to faith, "an auxiliary, the guiding
line of religious thought; it cannot be the integral object of
that thought."[2] And again, "Faith addresses itself to the
unchangeable truth, through a formula, necessarily inadequate,
capable of improvement, consequently of change."[3] Hence, in
Loisy's view, "The Church does not exact belief in its formulas
as the adequate expression of absolute truth, but presents them
as the least imperfect expression that is morally possible . . ."[4]

This view is based on a fundamental distinction between
"the material sense of the formula, the external image it presents," and "its proper religious and Christian significance,
its fundamental idea."[5] This is not necessarily to deny that
there is some unchangeable truth, but that seems to be beyond
human capability. "Such immutability is not compatible with
the nature of human intelligence. Our most certain knowledge
in the domains of nature and of science is always in movement,
always relative, always perfectible. It is not with the
elements of human thought that an everlasting edifice can be
built. Truth alone is unchangeable, but not its image in our
minds."[6] This paradigm of truth is vastly different from the
one outlined in the Roman School. Billot could understand this
only as complete relativism, as we have seen.[7]

[1]Loisy, The Gospel and the Church, pp. 210-11.

[2]Ibid., p. 224. [3]Ibid., pp. 217-18. [4]Ibid., p. 224.

[5]Ibid., p. 216. This reminds one of Newman's "Idea of
Christianity," supra, pp. 160.

[6]Loisy, The Gospel and the Church, p. 217.

[7]Supra, pp. "Billot."

The other distinction that enabled Loisy to deal with the anomalous situation was that between "truths of faith" and "truths of history." As Vidler explains it,

Thus, for instance, the divinity of Christ is a dogma of the church, and this means that Christ is God for faith. But the divinity of Christ is not a fact of history, nor would it be that even if Jesus Himself had taught it. It is a judgment of faith, made by the religious conscience. The historical process by which the dogma was formulated does not affect its truth, although it may suggest where its formulation is likely to need revision.[1]

But Vidler also points out that Loisy does not divorce these two kinds of truth though he distinguishes them. History is a description of events; dogma an appreciation of them.

Loisy also applied his evolutionary paradigm to the development of the church's cult and authority. Some form of authority is necessary in any society but the basically hierarchic structure of the church was to be found in the New Testament, not albeit in the form in which it is found today in the Roman Catholic church. "Thus to reproach the Catholic Church for the development of her constitution is to reproach her for having chosen to live, and that, moreover, when her life was indispensable for the preservation of the gospel itself."[2] He does not think, however, that the present centralized, authoritarian, juridical structure is the end of the developmental process. "The definitions of the Vatican (First Vatican Council) are to some extent sprung from reality; but if the centralizing tendency that led to it seems to have reached its limit, theological reflection has not yet spoken its final word on the subject. It is possible that the future will make observations on the true nature and object of the ecclesiastical

---

[1]Vidler, The Modernist Movement, p. 130.

[2]Loisy, The Gospel and the Church, p. 165.

158

authority, which cannot fail to react on the manner and conditions of its exercise."[1] He displays a similar justifying but
hopeful attitude toward the church's cult.

George Tyrrell, though trained in scholastic theology and
philosophy, is usually regarded as the mystic or prophetic
representative of the Modernists.[2] He was not the scholar that
Loisy was, but he was not theologically unsophisticated. Von
Hügel opened his mind to the problems raised by biblical and
historical studies, but these were not the source of his sense
of anomaly as they had been for Loisy. As Vidler remarks, "The
object of both modernists was the same, viz. to substitute for
the official theology one which took full account of the facts
of history as disclosed by criticism. But they followed a
different method just as they used a different terminology."[3]
Tyrrell was concerned with the experience of the Christian in
his "devotional life," the daily spiritual experience of the
average man as opposed to the problems of the scholar. It was
this relation of devotion to theology that focused the area of
anomaly for Tyrrell. "Devotion and religion existed before
theology, in the way that art existed before art-criticism;
reasoning, before logic; speech, before grammar. . . . theology,
as far as it is true to the life of faith and charity as
actually lived, so far is it a law and corrective for all. But
when it begins to contradict the facts of that spiritual life,
it loses its reality and its authority; and needs itself to be
corrected by the lex orandi."[4] The lex orandi is the criterion

[1]Ibid., p. 210.

[2]Vidler, The Modernist Movement, p. 142; M.D. Petre,
Modernism: Its Failure and Its Fruits (London: T.C. & E.C. Jack,
Ltd., 1918), p. 224.

[3]Vidler, The Modernist Movement, p. 166.

[4]George Tyrrell, Through Scylla and Charybdis (London:
Longmans, Green and Co., 1907), p. 105.

for the <u>lex credendi</u>. The facts that must be dealt with for

Tyrrell are not the facts revealed by scholarly research

(though he is not about to deny these) but the facts of

experience. He says,

> . . . liberal theology, like natural science, has for its subject-matter a certain ever-present department of human experience which it endeavors progressively to formulate and understand, and which is ever at hand to furnish a criterion of the success of such endeavours; whereas our school-divinity finds its subject-matter in the record or register of certain past experiences that cannot be repeated and are known to us only through such a record . . . We do not ask if Copernican be true to Ptolemaic astronomy, but if it be true to experience. Nor does the liberal theologian ask or care that his theology be substantially identical with that of the past, but only that it be truer to experience than that which it supersedes.[1]

As is clear, Tyrrell was reacting against the scholastic

theology (for that is what he means by theology)[2] in which he

had been trained. He makes a distinction between theology and

revelation. It is theology that develops and changes, not

revelation. Revelation and theology are "generically different

orders of Truth and Knowledge." He explains it thus:

> It is plain, then, that there is a generic difference between Revelational and Theological truth, and that they cannot be compared as two statements--poetic and scientific --of the same fact. "Prophetic" truth cannot be used, as statements can be used from which we may deduce other statements. Revelation is a showing on the part of God, a seeing on the part of the receiver. Prophecy is but the communication of this vision to others. Theology must take prophecy not as statement, but as experience; must try to understand it as a religious phenomenon, and use it as factual not as verbal evidence for its conceptual constructions of the supernatural order.[3]

Theology is implicit in revelation as theory is implicit in

experience. The revelation does not change or develop.[4] But

that is because revelation for Tyrrell is an "idea" in Newman's

sense of the word.[5] It is a "concrete end, whose realization is

---

[1]Tyrrell, <u>Through Scylla and Charybdis</u>, p. 136.

[2]<u>Ibid.</u>, p. 86. [3]<u>Ibid.</u>, pp. 86, 289. [4]<u>Ibid.</u>, pp. 4-5.

[5]Vidler, <u>20th Century Defenders</u>, p. 48; George Tyrrell, <u>Christianity at the Crossroads</u> (London: Longmans, Green, and Co., 1910), pp. 62, 271.

160

the term of a process of action and endeavour. It is akin to
that Augustinian _notio_ (or _ratio_) _seminalis_, with which every
living germ seems to be animated, and which works itself out to
full expression through a process of growth and development. It
does not change in itself, but is the cause of change in its
embodiment."[1] Thus Tyrrell deals with the anomaly raised by
history and experience for theology and dogmatic statements by
locating change in theology, (rational theology, i.e.), while
at the same time insisting that the apostolic revelation has an
"unchanging, unprogressive character."[2] He seeks in this way to
guide his way between Scylla and Charybdis--the former being the
error of the old theology with its unchanging dogma, and the
latter the new (Liberal Protestantism) theology of a merely
evolutionary process lacking anything permanent.[3] At the same
time he deals with the results of scientific and historical
criticism by allowing theology to confront this challenge while
removing revelation (the idea of Jesus as the Divine indwelling
and saving Spirit--the very essence of Christianity)[4] from the
field of battle.

It is not necessary nor to the point here to evaluate how
successful was the attempt of the Modernists to come to terms
with the anomalous situation as they saw it in the early part of
this century. Our only point is that there was such an attempt;
that there was a challenge to the paradigms dominant in the
"official" theology of the Roman School; that it was strongly
and even harshly rejected by the spokesmen for the profession;
that there were novel theories of "revelation," "dogma,"

[1]Tyrrell, _Christianity at the Crossroads_, p. 62.
[2]Tyrrell, _Through Scylla and Charybdis_, pp. 4-5.
[3]Vidler, _The Modernist Movement_, p. 173.
[4]Tyrrell, _Christianity at the Crossroads_, p. 271.

"deposit of faith," "theology" and "faith" advanced in an
attempt to deal with the sources of anomaly--historical awareness and, to a lesser extent, the emerging pluralism. All of
which parallel Kuhn's description of symptoms of "crisis" in
science.

Vatican II and the Current Alternatives

As we have pointed out (supra, p. 143) anomaly may be
recognized at first only by a restricted segment of the professional community and we have suggested that Newman and the
Modernists are examples of this characteristic in the case of
the developing crisis of the magisterium. At the Second
Vatican Council the awareness and recognition of the anomaly
burst forth in many ways, sufficient for us to say that most of
the outstanding men in the discipline were concerned with the
problem-area. Indeed, the Council has been described as a conflict between the non-historical theology of the Roman School
and the new theologies characterized by their historical
consciousness.[1] The problem of pluralism was also of great concern, much more so than for Newman or the Modernists.[2]

I have used Vatican II as a terminus for this study, not
because the process of shifting paradigms is complete, but
because it served to expose publicly the deficiencies of the
paradigms of the previously dominant theology and, to some
extent at least, unseat them from the chairs of dogmatic
theology. Indeed, Vatican II is an excellent example of the
actual process of shifting paradigms, compressed in time. For
despite the fact that the older models, as represented in the

---

[1] Michael Novak, The Open Church (New York: The Macmillan
Company, 1964), pp. 52 ff., esp. p. 66; and John Courtney Murray
in private conversations with the author.

[2] Evidenced by the concern for relations with Protestants,
Jews, and Orthodox as well as a consideration for and influence
of their theologies on the Council documents.

162

schema on the church first presented to the council by the
preparatory Theological Commission, were rejected and criticized,
they were still strong enough in the minds of some to be present
in the Dogmatic Constitution that was eventually adopted. The
shift in paradigms is still going on, and the documents of
Vatican II contain several models side by side. They are clearly
compromise documents and no one model dominates. George Lindbeck has criticized the documents of the Council for this
ambiguity and lack of unity.[1]

Of the paradigms immediately involved in the notion of the
magisterium, that of truth and, because of its close relationship to the question of truth, that of teaching did not shift
perceptibly. The Second Vatican Council accepted almost without
question the paradigm of truth of the Roman School, as Küng
points out in his recent book on infallibility.[2] On the other
hand, the models of the socio-political structure of the church
and of the forms of authority in it did shift somewhat. They
shifted in the sense that more than one model is present in the
documents, not that one model has replaced another. The juridical, hierarchical model that we have described in the Roman
School is still present, though it is not as dominant as the
others. Some of its implications appear in Chapter III in the
reaffirmation of the papal prerogatives and in the discussion
of the relation of the bishops as a college to the pope; but
the model itself was repudiated in the Council. Congar says
that the Council "went from a predominantly juridical conception
to the primacy of the ontology of grace, from a predominance of

---

[1]George Lindbeck, The Future of Roman Catholic Theology
(Philadelphia: Fortress Press, 1970), pp. 12 ff.

[2]Hans Küng, Infallible? An Inquiry, trans. by Edward Quinn
(Garden City, J.J.: Doubleday & Company, Inc., 1971), pp. 72,
152.

system to the affirmation of Christian man," and Charles Moeller one of the architects of the schema, agrees.[1]

The second ecclesiological model that had been parallel with but never integrated into the juridical model of the Roman School was that of the Mystical Body of Christ. We have seen that the early founders of the Roman School had an ecclesiology characterized as a "Mystical Body Theology," but that it had fallen by the wayside until the early part of the twentieth century when it was taken up and developed by such men as Karl Adam, Romano Guardini and Emile Mersch, and, under the influence of Sebatian Tromp, culminated in the encyclical Mystici corporis by Pius XII in 1943. This model had the advantage of stressing the function of the sacraments and the life of grace in the church as well as the varying positions of clergy and laity in "building up the body of Christ" (Lumen gentium (Ch. I, p. 20, n. 7). But it does not sufficiently integrate the inner and outer realities of the church, and so Lumen gentium cautioned that "the society furnished with hierarchical agencies and the Mystical Body of Christ are not to be considered as two realities, nor are the visible assembly and the spiritual community. . . ."[3] It was precisely this criticism of the Mystical Body model that led to the third, and I think, dominant ecclesiological model of the Council documents, the "pilgrim People of God" model.

The "pilgrim People of God" model was put forth in the first document the Council produced, the Constitution on the Sacred Liturgy, and had its source in the renewed biblical and

[1]Yves Congar, "The People of God," and Charles Moeller, "History of Lumen Gentium's Structure and Ideas," both in Vatican II: An Interfaith Appraisal, ed. by John H. Miller (Notre Dame, Indiana: University of Notre Dame Press, 1966), p. 143 and passim.

[3]Lumen Gentium, Ch. I, 8, p. 22.

liturgical studies. Its imagery is founded in the Exodus
narrative of the Old Testament and has several characteristics
that overcome the deficiencies of the other two models. First,
a people is a visible society and as such requires structure,
and offices and authority. This model provides a base for
thinking about the external, visible character of the church
without being legalistic or juridical about it. It enabled the
Council to stress authority in the church as service rather than
dominance. Secondly, the awareness of the church as a community
which the liturgical movement had fostered and which was one of
the advantages of the Mystical Body model is emphasized in this
model as well. At the beginning of Chapter II, the Council says
that "It has pleased God, however, to make men holy and save
them not merely as individuals without any mutual bonds, but by
making them into a single people, a people which acknowledges
Him in truth and serves Him in holiness."[1] This model incor-
porates the historical perspective insofar as the People of God
is still making its way through history subject to the viscis-
situdes and vagaries thereof, not yet having achieved its goal,
the kingdom, and, hence, still in need of purification and
reform. This is in distinct contrast to the former paradigm
of the church already identifiable with Christ, sharing in his
glory and triumph. It presents an image of a church that shares
the suffering and humiliation of its Founder, "Moving forward
through trial and tribulation, the Church is strengthened by
the power of God's grace promised her by the Lord, so that in
the weakness of the flesh she may not waver from perfect
fidelity, but remain a bride worthy of her Lord; that moved by
the Holy Spirit she may never cease to renew herself, until
through the cross she arrives at the light which knows no setting.[2]

---

[1] Lumen Gentium, Ch. II, 9, p. 25.

[2] Ibid., p. 26.

This latter paradigm of the structure of the church had some bearing on and provided some foundation for the other significant paradigm shift in authority--to a more collegial notion. The basis for this was the communal sense of responsibility involved in the People of God model of a covenant theology as opposed to the more individualistic orientation of the juridical model or the Head-Body relationship of the Mystical Body paradigm. But an affirmation of collegiality on all levels has appeared side by side with a repetition of the papal prerogative of Vatican I.[1] Küng suggests that this merely extended the idea of papal infallibility of Vatican I to the episcopate as a whole.[2]

It is not our intention to do a detailed survey or analysis of Vatican II, but merely to indicate that the multiple paradigms evident in the documents may be understood as a phase of the process of shifting from one set of paradigms to another; that the process was not completed with the Council; but that the Council did theologically at least (whether or not practically remains to be seen) dislodge the previously dominant paradigms of the socio-political structure of the church, and, to a lesser extent perhaps, the paradigm of authority that had prevailed in the Roman School.

Vatican II did not form a new consensus among theologians on the paradigms that would dominate their future thinking about the magisterium. If anything, it produced further investigation into the problem-areas pointed out by the historical consciousness and the awareness of religious and cultural pluralism. Karl Rahner, for example, has been increasingly preoccupied since the Council with both of these factors--the historicity of the church and of her teachings, and the

[1] Repeated practically verbatim in par. 25.
[2] Küng, Infallible?, p. 138.

166

pluralistic situation in which she finds herself in the world
as well as pluralism in theology itself. In his usual thought-
ful and moderate way, he suggests that there must be a _via media_
for the magisterium between what he calls a "Pian monolith"--a
policy followed from the time of Pius IX "for which everything
was clear, or in any case everything important could easily,
unambiguously and, above all, quickly be decided, and also was
decided by some form of papal declaration. . . ."--and a policy
of "bewildering confusion in which theologians and laymen think
that they can say and think anything they want in matters of
faith."[1] For him the "church must have a confession of faith"
and a "teaching office which can express the faith of the church
truly, in genuine human concepts, and binding on all."[2] Nevertheless, the two sources of anomaly impose limitations on the
magisterium as it will have to function in the future. Rahner
recognizes that, "Doctrine really has a history and a development which cannot be explained merely as the acquisition of new
and additional knowledge. Rather, the old, "immutable" truths
are understood in a new way," and that the magisterium cannot
"impose an absolutely homogeneous theology" on the theological
world.[3] This pluralism in theology is due to the analogous
nature of concepts in which the magisterium must express itself.[4]
He says, accurately I believe,

> The limitation of every metaphysical-theological expression
> and the impossibility of ever concluding the process of
> interpretation has dawned on the Church only since 1870 or
> is dawning now. This realization makes any 'new' definition
> already 'old' from the start; that is, the moment it appears,

---

[1]Karl Rahner, "Theology and the Magisterium after the
Council," _Theology Digest_, Sesquicentennial Issue, 1968, pp. 6-7.

[2]Ibid. [3]Ibid., pp. 8-9.

[4]Karl Rahner, "A Century of Infallibility," _Theology Digest_,
XVIII, 3 (August, 1970), 220.

it is confronted with such a number of possible interpretations that it brings no real 'progress' in clarifying previous dogmas.[1]

The consequences of this theological pluralism for the teaching authority in the future are significant. He compares the attitudes reflected in Humani generis (1950) with the letter of Cardinal Ottaviani of July, 1966:

> In the former, the attitude that still pervades throughout is that the adversary's position can be formulated unambiguously and the official position of the Church can be clearly differentiated from it in a positive statement. In the latter, the feeling is more that of being somewhat at a loss in the face of tendencies in theology that cannot be quite pinned down, cannot be manipulated and reduced to a common understanding. Hence, the result is questions and general warnings rather than explicit teachings.[2]

In a state of theological pluralism, it is extremely difficult if not impossible for one exercising the teaching authority in the church to know the presuppositions of a particular theology, and hence it would be (ideally speaking) necessary to have as many "teaching offices" as there are theologies.[3]

As Rahner himself admits, he does better at formulating the problem than at offering a solution. But he is immensely aware of the historicity of truth. He does not have the immutable deposit of faith paradigm. "We are involved in history and only in this ongoing process do we possess the eternal truth of God which is our salvation. The truth retains its identity which has a history and continues to have one. We always have this same, identical truth, but never in such a way that we could detach it completely from its historical form."[4]

---

[1]Rahner, "A Century of Infallibility," p. 221.

[2]Karl Rahner, "Philosophy and Philosophizing in Theology," Theology Digest, Sesquicentennial Issue, 1968, p. 27.

[3]Ibid.

[4]Karl Rahner, "The Historical Dimension in Theology," Theology Digest, Sesquicentennial Issue, 1968, p. 35.

Along with this awareness, he places greater emphasis on the
responsibility of the local bishops for teaching. "The bishops
cannot simply pass this responsibility on to the Roman Congregations nor to the thelogians."[1] In effect, he espouses the
principle of subsidiarity in the teaching office. In consequence of the pluralistic situation of theology, he affirms the
necessity of dialogue rather than the paradigm of truth being
handed down from above.[2]

All of these emphases in Rahner's post-conciliar reflections arise in the light of the "pilgrim People of God" model
of the church which he feels is the theme of the whole constitution on the church.[3] His image of authority in the church is
that of service, rather than domination. His paradigm of truth
is historical and limited, fragmentary and always liable to
further perfection. His image of teaching is that of dialogue
rather than of a master-pupil relationship. The relationship
between truth and history he considers one of the basic problems of philosophy, but does not essay a solution. He is perhaps wiser in this regard than the other major figure in contemporary ecclesiology whose thought we will mention briefly
here, Hans Küng.

---

[1]Rahner, "Theology and the Magisterium . . . ," p. 10.

[2]Ibid., and his essay, "Reflections on Dialogue within
a Pluralistic Society," Theological Investigations, VI, trans.
by Karl-H. and Boniface Kruger (Baltimore: Helicon Press,
1969), 31ff.

[3]Karl Rahner, "The Sinful Church in the Decrees of
Vatican II," Theological Investigations, VI, 281.

Küng's latest book, Infallible? An Inquiry, which has
already caused quite a reaction,[1] is consistent with his previous work and builds on it. It will serve as a sufficient
summary of his point of view on the magisterium and the alternate paradigms he offers. His interest is much the same as
ours insofar as he is aware of the "crisis" with regard to the
magisterium. The "ecclesiastical 'teaching office' is conceived by the Pope and also by a number of bishops largely in
a preconciliar authoritarian way" and, "No one has done more in
recent years to provoke the demythologizing of the ecclesiastical teaching office than this teaching office itself."[2]

Beginning his reflections, as we did, with the crisis
precipitated by Humanae vitae, Küng suggests that we should
cease trying by theological maneuvering to justify previous
mistakes of the magisterium and admit that "infallibility" can
apply only to God, not to any specific man-made propositions.
The "infallibility" of the church is not dependent on individually infallible propositions, yet this is the presupposition
(albeit unexamined) of both Vatican I and Vatican II.[3] Küng
focuses more than Rahner on the problematic nature of all propositions: They always fall short of reality; they are necessarily open to misunderstanding; they can only be translated

---

[1]For some critical reviews at the time of this writing,
cf. Gregory Baum, Commonweal, April 9, 1971, pp. 103-05; David
Tracy, The Christian Century, May 19, 1971, pp. 631-33; the
symposium in America, April 24, 1971; Avery Dulles, "Theological
Issues," Michael A. Fahey, "Europe's Theologians Join the Debate"
George A. Lindbeck, "A Protestant Perspective."

[2]Küng, Infallible?, pp. 13-14.

[3]Ibid., pp. 151-53.

up to a point; they are always in motion; and they are
"ideology-prone."[1] Propositions of faith share these limitations. He also points out, as we have, the Cartesian-rational-
istic notion of truth that underlay the theology of the Roman
School and the Vatican Councils in which clarity and distinct-
ness "were made the criterion of truth, while truth itself was
identified with certainty."[2] The problematic nature of propositions leads him to say not only that propositions can be true
or false but that they can be both true and false.[3] There are
so many possible sources of error that it is impossible to say
that any proposition is in principle free from error. Hence,
propositions cannot be infallible. Yet we do have the promises
of Christ (Mt 16:17, 28:20, Jn 14:16, 16:13, I Tim 3:15).

Küng does not want either to deny the promises of Christ
or to deny errors on the part of the magisterium. His solution
is to "raise the alternatives to a higher plane: The Church
will persist in the truth IN SPITE OF all ever possible
errors!"[4] Thus the infallibility of the church is really indefectibility or perpetuity in truth--a fundamental remaining
of the church in truth, which is not annulled by individual
errors.[5] His answer to the question of the book is put thus:

_____

[1]Küng, Infallible?, pp. 157-61.

[2]Ibid., pp. 165-67.

[3]Ibid., p. 170. For a critique of this position see
Lindbeck's article listed above.

[4]Küng, Infallible?, p. 175.

[5]Ibid., pp. 181-82.

God alone is infallible in the strict sense of the
term. He alone is a priori free from error (immunis
ab errore) in detail and indeed in every case: he is
therefore the one who a priori can neither deceive
nor be deceived. The Church, however, composed of
human beings, which is not God and never becomes God,
can constantly and in a very human way deceive herself
and others on every plane and in all spheres. Therefore, in order to avoid all misunderstanding, it is
better to ascribe to the Church, not 'infallibility,'
but--on the basis of faith in the promises--'indefectibility' or 'perpetuity': an unshatterability
and indestructibility, in brief, a fundamental remaining in the truth in spite of all ever possible
errors.[1]

What, then, is this truth which cannot be captured in

propositions but in which the church remains? It is the "truth

of the gospel of Jesus Christ" which, like the Spirit   the

church has received, is a pledge, a promise "which calls her

out on to the road, into that future which alone will bring the

whole truth, the complete revelation, the kingdom of God."[2]

It is not something possessed once-and-for-all in a "deposit,"

but something to be approached asymtotically, never to be en-

capsulated in human language. He recalls the Scriptural notion

of truth as fidelity, constancy, relaibility[3] and speaks of

the direction of the church, so that truth seems to be the

fidelity in the pursuit of something not yet achieved rather

than the secure possession of something previously given. This

is obviously a paradigm of truth quite different from that of

the Roman School and of Pope Paul VI!

I have concentrated on Küng's paradigm of truth because

that is what is most distinctive in this important book. His

---

[1]Küng, Infallible? p. 185.

[2]Ibid., p. 178.

[3]Ibid., pp. 186, 220.

172

historical and biblical arguments had been presented previously[1] and are shared by a number of Roman Catholic theologians.

His view of the teaching office as not limited to bishops and

as being one of service rather than domination,[2] his insistence

on the need for dialogue and participation of all members of

the Christian community and his call for honesty and truthful-

ness in the face of historical scholarship, are shared by many.

Those two words, dialogue and participation, are descrip-

tive of the paradigm of authority that is operative for a num-

ber of contemporary Roman Catholic theologians. For example,

Gregory Baum says that:

> Vatican II acknowledges the effect of man's new self-
> understanding of his social organizations by making
> participation the key concept for all institutional
> changes. . . . The collegial authority of the bishops
> is neither potestas ordinis nor potestas jurisdictionis.
> It is the acknowledgement of team responsibility that
> transcends the traditional understanding of power in
> the Catholic Church. The dialogue structure in the
> exercise of authority is acknowledged for every level
> of the ecclesiastical institution.[3]

Avery Dulles uses a metaphor to summarize similar ideas--the

light of the Gospel and of the Spirit is diffused throughout

the total church among individuals and groups which are differ-

ently gifted, and the function of the bishops and pope is to be

a lens by which this radiance of light is gathered up and

---

[1]His previous books, Structures of the Church, trans. by
Salvator Attanasio (New York: Thomas Nelson & Sons, 1964); The
Church, trans. by Ray and Rosaleen Ockenden (New York: Sheed &
Ward, 1967); Truthfulness: the Future of the Church, trans. by
Edward Quinn (New York: Sheed & Ward, 1968).

[2]Küng, Infallible?, pp. 229-30.

[3]Gregory Baum, The Credibility of the Church Today (New
York: Herder & Herder, 1968), pp. 188-89.

173

brought to focus.[1] The truth taught has its sources in a
broad base and only its expression at a central point. The
pyramidal model has been reversed. The function of authority
in this paradigm is not to command as the sole legal spokesman
for the divine will, but to summarize and express the consensus
that is discovered to exist in the community as a whole. To
discover this requires dialogue and participation by many,
those holding office and those not, those with knowledge of
different disciplines, and those with different life-experi-
ences.

We have not been attempting to survey contemporary Roman
Catholic ecclesiology. We have merely indicated that at present there are alternative paradigms being proffered for consideration. These must now be tested, according to Kuhn, both
against one another and against the experience available to the
community.[2] This in itself requires dialogue and that demands
the exposition and articulation of the paradigms involved.

It has been the purpose of this thesis to contribute to
an understanding of the current disagreement about the nature
and function of the teaching authority in the Christian community by exposing the paradigms operative in the theology of the
Roman School. We have only briefly indicated the other paradigms available. We dare not venture to predict what the
ultimate choice of the theological community will be. We do
believe that the anomalous situation is too pressing for the old
paradigms ever to regain their dominant position. For the
choice is not just between abstract theologies but, as Kuhn has
said, between "incompatible modes of community life."

---

[1]Avery Dulles, The Survival of Dogma (Garden City, N. Y.:
Doubleday & Company, Inc., 1971), pp. 106-07.

[2]Kuhn, The Structure of Scientific Revolutions, p. 145.

Concluding Reflections on Theology and Crisis

We have investigated the crisis of the magisterium in the light of Kuhn's theory of paradigm change and explained the present status of the disagreement as part of the process of shifting from one set of paradigms to another. It was not our purpose in the thesis to do any more than that. But one may ask the question of what value such an approach is to the field of theology as a whole. Are there other instances of such paradigm shifts beside the one we have chosen, or is it an isolated example? Without having done a similar amount of research on other topics, I cannot answer that question definitively; I would, however, venture to suggest that the specific areas mentioned previously, namely, birth control and celibacy of the clergy, also focus the crisis of the magisterium and could, therefore, profitably be analyzed in the manner suggested. Likewise, although one cannot say that a crisis is upon us in these areas, the future of the theology of the Eucharist, Christology, and what used to be referred to as the problem of "nature and grace" could usefully employ Kuhn's categories.

Wherein lies the profit or the use? First of all, the difficulty of communication between those operating on diverse paradigms (supra, p. 109) can be somewhat overcome by explicating and articulating the paradigms as best one can. The attempt to understand the other point of view is always necessary for dialogue. If we are going to have to live with pluralism in theology as Rahner and Schillebeeck suggest (supra, p. 167-68, Ch. V), then this explicitation and articulation will be a fundamental function of theology in the future. It is a necessary service to the Christian community.

Secondly, it seems to be a suitable means for freeing
theology from its ideological component and carrying on that
self-corrective process of freeing it from its biases and
prejudices that we mentioned at the beginning (supra, p. 6).
If I may cite Baum again,

> There is no objective point of view, abstract and
> superior, from which questions may be asked. For
> this reason the theologian must make explicit for
> himself the reasons for his choice of questions,
> submit them to a theological critique, and either by
> keeping, modifying or rejecting them, assume responsi-
> bility for the political meaning of his choice.[1]

It seems to me that paradigm analysis is a way of doing just
this. The political consequences of any theological position
need to be explored, and understanding and explicitating the
paradigms that are involved in that theology is a step toward
this.

Thirdly, there is no doubt that we are in need of a
theology of change. I do not say "development" because we need
to face the fact of change as it is without minimizing it or
hiding it by convoluted theological manuevering. Our historical awareness forces this kind of honesty upon us. Kuhn's
theory of paradigm shifts may provide such an understanding.
This would be in contrast to a theory of accumulation in which
the Christian community adds more and more insights without
ever losing any of the "truth" already accumulated, as well as
in contrast to a theory of explicitation in which truth once
possessed comes to even greater clarity and explicitness (such
as Billot and the Roman School generally held). There is no
particular reason why a theory of change which is verifiable in
other disciplines may not also be true of theology. It cannot

---

[1] Baum, "Theology and Ideology," p. 27.

be assumed to be accurate, however, without a considerable
amount of historical research. Hence, it is only a possible
area of investigation, not a substantiated generalization.
This, along with the socio-cultural sources of the paradigms,
are areas which this thesis leaves for further pursuit.

BIBLIOGRAPHY

Books

Abbott, Walter M., ed., The Documents of Vatican II. New York: Guild Press, 1966.

Adam, Karl. The Spirit of Catholicism, trans. by Justin McCann. New York: The Macmillan Co., 1929.

Adolfs, Robert. The Grave of God, trans. by N. D. Smith. New York: Harper & Row, Publishers, 1967.

Altholz, Josef L. The Churches in the Nineteenth Century. New York: Bobbs-Merrill Co., Inc., 1967.

Arévalo, Catalino G. "Some Aspects of the Theology of the Mystical Body of Christ in the Ecclesiology of Giovanni Perrone, Carlo Passaglia and Clemens Schrader." (Unpublished dissertation from Pontificia Universitas Gregoriana, Rome, 1959.) Excerpts published at Rome: Pontificia Universitas Gregoriana, 1959.

Aubert, Roger. La Pontificat de Pie IX (1846-1878). Paris: Bloud & Gay, 1952.

Auricchio, John. The Future of Theology. Staten Island, New York: Alba House, 1970.

Baum, Gregory. The Credibility of the Church Today. New York: Herder & Herder, 1968.

Bellamy, Jean. La Théologie Catholique au XIXe Siècle. Paris: Gabriel Beauchesne & Co., 1904.

Berger, Peter L. and Thomas Luckmann. The Social Construction of Reality. New York: Doubleday & Company, Inc., Anchor Books, 1967.

Biemer, Günter. Newman on Tradition, trans. by and edited by Kevin Smyth. New York: Herder & Herder, 1967.

Billot, Louis Cardinal. De Ecclesia Christi. 3rd ed. Prati: Ciachetti, Filii et Soc., 1909.

_____. De immutabilitate traditionis contra modernam haeresim evolutionismi. Rome: Gregorian University Press, 1904, 1929.

Billot, Louis Cardinal. Liberalism: The Satanic Social Solvent. Translated by G. B. O'Toole. Beatty, Pa.: The Archabbey Press, 1922.

Bouyer, Louis. Newman. Translated by J. Lewis May. Cleveland: Meridian, 1960.

Brinton, Crane. The Shaping of Modern Thought. Englewood
Cliffs, N. J.: Prentice-Hall, 1963.

Burtchaell, James T. Catholic Theories of Biblical Inspiration
since 1810. Cambridge: The University Press, 1969.

Bury, John B. History of the Papacy in the 19th Century (1864-
1878). London: Macmillan & Co., 1930.

Butler, Christopher. The Idea of the Church. Baltimore:
Helicon Press, 1962.

Butler, Cuthbert. The Vatican Council: 1869-1870. Edited by
Christopher Butler, Westminster: The Newman Press, 1962.

Butler, Edward Cuthbert. The Vatican Council. 2 Vols. London: Longmans, Green, 1930.

Callahan, Daniel, ed. The Catholic Case for Contraception.
New York: The Macmillan Company, 1969.

_____, Oberman, Heiko A., and O'Hanlon, Daniel J.,
eds. Christianity Divided. New York: Sheed & Ward, 1961.

Chadwick, Owen. From Bossuet to Newman. The Idea of Doctrinal
Development. Cambridge: The University Press, 1957.

Congar, Yves M.-J. A History of Theology. Translated and
edited by Hunter Guthrie, S.J. New York: Doubleday and
Company, Inc., 1968.

_____. The Meaning of Tradition. Translated by A. N.
Woodrow. New York: Hawthorn Books, 1964.

_____. Tradition and Traditions. New York: Macmillan,
1967.

_____. Vraie et Fausse Reforme dans l'Eglise. Paris:
Editions du Cerf, 1950.

Connolly, James M. The Voices of France. New York: The
Macmillan Co., 1961.

Curran, Charles, ed. Contraception: Authority and Dissent.
New York: Herder & Herder, 1969.

Curran, Charles, and Hunt, Robert E. Dissent In and For the
Church: Theologians and Humanae Vitae. New York: Sheed &
Ward, 1969.

DeLubac, Henri. The Splendour of the Church. Translated by
Michael Mason. New York: Sheed & Ward, 1956.

Deneffe, August. Der Traditionsbegriff. Studie zur Theologie.
Munster: Aschendorffsche Verlagsbuchhandlung, 1931.

Dewart, Leslie. Religion, Language and Truth. New York:
Herder & Herder, 1970.

Dibble, Romuald A. John Henry Newman: The Concept of Infallible Doctrinal Authority. Unpublished dissertation, The
Catholic University of America, 1955.

Dru, Alexander. The Contribution of German Catholicism. New York: Hawthorn Books, 1963.

Dulles, Avery. The Survival of Dogma. Garden City, New York: Doubleday & Company, Inc., 1971.

Fawkes, Alfred. Studies in Modernism. London: Smith, Elder & Co., 1913.

Femiano, Samuel D. Infallibility of the Laity. New York: Herder & Herder, 1967.

Flanagan, Donald, ed. The Evolving Church. Staten Island, New York: Alba House, 1966.

Forsyth, Peter T. The Principal of Authority. London: Hodder & Staughton.

Franzelin, John Baptist. De Divina Traditione et Scriptura. 3rd ed. Rome: S. C. de Propaganda Fide, 1882.

_____. De Ecclesia Christi. Rome: S. C. de Propaganda Fide, 1887.

Geiselmann, Josef R. The Meaning of Tradition. New York: Herder & Herder, 1966.

Gilkey, Langdon. Naming the Whirlwind: The Renewal of God-Language. New York: Bobbs-Merrill Company, 1969.

Grønbech, Vilhelm. Religious Currents in the Nineteenth Century. Lawrence: The University of Kansas Press, 1964.

De Guibert, Joseph. De Christi Ecclesia. 2nd ed. Rome: Gregorian University Press, 1928.

Hales, E. E. Y. The Catholic Church in the Modern World. New York: Image Paperback, 1960.

_____. Revolution and Papacy, 1796-1846. London, 1960.

Halperin, S. William. Italy and the Vatican at War. A Study of Their Relations from the Outbreak of the Franco-Prussian War to the Death of Pius IX. Chicago: The University of Chicago Press, 1939.

_____. The Separation of Church and State in Italian Thought from Cavour to Mussolini. Chicago: The University of Chicago Press, 1937.

Hamer, Jerome. The Church is a Communion. New York: Sheed & Ward, 1964.

Hanson, R. P. C. Tradition in the Early Church. Philadelphia: Westminster Press, 1963.

Hayes, Carlton J. H. Contemporary Europe Since 1870. New York: Macmillan Co., 1953.

Heaney, John J. The Modernist Crisis: von Hügel. London: Geoffrey Chapman, 1969.

180

Hennesey, James J. The First Council of the Vatican. New
York: Herder & Herder, 1963.

Hocedez, Edgar. Histoire de la Théologie au XIXe Siècle.
3 vols. Paris: Desclee de Brouwer, 1947-52.

Holstein, Henri. La Tradition dans l'Eglise. Paris, 1960.

Hunt, John F. and Terrence R. Connelly. The Responsibility of
Dissent: The Church and Academic Freedom. New York:
Sheed & Ward, 1969.

Jaki, Stanislas. Les Tendances nouvelles de l'Ecclésiologie.
Rome: Casa Editrice Herder, 1957.

Journet, Charles. The Church of the Word Incarnate, trans. by
A. H. C. Downes. Vol. 1: The Apostolic Hierarchy. New
York: Sheed & Ward, 1955.

_____. Esquisse du Developpment du Dogme marial.
Paris: Alsatia, 1954.

Kasper, Walter. Dogma unter dem Wort Gottes. Mainz: Matthias-
Grunewald-Verlag, 1965.

_____. Die Lehre von der Tradition in der Römischen
Schule (Giovanni Perrone, Carlo Passaglia, Clemens
Schrader). Freiburg: Herder, 1962.

Kuhn, Thomas S. The Structure of Scientific Revolutions.
Chicago: The University of Chicago Press, 1962.

Küng, Hans. The Church, trans. by Ray and Rosaleen Ockenden.
New York: Sheed & Ward, 1967.

_____. Infallible? An Inquiry, trans. by Edward
Quinn. Garden City, New York: Doubleday & Company, Inc.
1971.

_____. Structures of the Church, trans. by Salvator
Attanasio. New York: Thomas Nelson & Sons, 1964.

_____. Truthfulness: The Future of the Church, trans.
by Edward Quinn. New York: Sheed & Ward, 1968.

Van Laak, Herman. Institutiones Theologiae Fundamentalis. Rome:
Gregorian University Press, 1908-11.

Lakatos, Imre and Alan Musgrave, eds., Criticism and the Growth
of Knowledge. Proceedings of the International Colloquium
in the Philosophy of Science, London, 1965, Vol. IV.
Cambridge: The University Press, 1970.

Latourette, Kenneth Scott. Christianity in a Revolutionary Age.
Vols. I-III. New York: Harper & Brothers, Publishers,
1958.

Laubacher, James A. Dogma and the Development of Dogma in the
Writings of George Tyrrell. Dissertation. Louvain, 1939.

Lee, Anthony D., ed., Vatican II: The Theological Dimension.
N. C.: The Thomist Press, 1963.

Lilley, A. Leslie. Modernism, A Record and Review. London: Pitman & Sons, 1908.

Lindbeck, George A. The Future of Roman Catholic Theology. Philadelphia: The Fortress Press, 1970.

Loisy, Alfred. Autour d'Un Petit Livre. 2nd ed. Paris: Alphonse Picard et Fils, 1903.

_____. The Gospel and the Church, trans. by Christopher Home. New York: Charles Scribner's Sons, 1912.

_____. Mémoires pour Servir à l'Histoire Religieuse de Notre Temps. 3 vols. Paris: Emile Nourry, 1930-31.

_____. My Duel with the Vatican, trans. by Richard W. Boynton. New York: E. P. Dutton & Co., 1924.

Löwith, Karl. From Hegel to Nietzsche. New York: Holt, Rinehart and Winston, 1964.

McBrien, Richard P. Church: The Continuing Quest. New York: Newman Press, 1970.

_____. Do We Need the Church? New York: Harper & Row, Publishers, 1969.

McDonald, Hugh D. Theories of Revelation. London: George Allen & Unwin, Ltd., 1963.

McKenzie, John L. Authority in the Church. New York: Sheed & Ward, 1966.

McNamara, Kevin, ed., Vatican II: The Constitution on the Church. London: Geoffrey Chapman, 1968.

Mackey, J. P. Modern Theology of Tradition. New York: Herder & Herder, 1963.

Mazzella, Camillus Cardinal. De Religione et Ecclesia. 5th ed. Rome: Forzani et Socii, 1896.

Mersche, Emile. The Whole Christ, trans. by John R. Kelly. Milwaukee: The Bruce Publishing Co., 1938.

Miller, John H. Vatican II: An Interfaith Appraisal. International Theological Conference, University of Notre Dame, March 20-26, 1966. Notre Dame, Indiana: University of Notre Dame Press, 1966.

Möhler, Johann A. Die mündliche Überlieferung. Beitrage zum Begriff der Tradition, ed. by M. Schmaus. Munich: Herder, 1957.

_____. Symbolism: Or an Exposition of the Doctrinal Differences between Catholics and Protestants as Evidenced by their Symbolical Writings, trans. by James Burton Robertson. 2 vols. 2nd ed. London: Charles Dolman, 1847.

182

Moody, Joseph N., ed., Church and Society, Catholic Social and
    Political Thought and Movements, 1789-1950. New York:
    Arts, Inc., 1953.

Moran, Gabriel. Scripture and Tradition: A Survey of the Con-
    troversy. New York: Herder & Herder, 1963.

Nédoncelle, Maurice, et al. L'Ecclésiologie au XIXe Siècle.
    Unam Sanctam 34. Colloque de la Faculté de Théologie
    Catholique de Strasbourg. Paris: Editions du Cerf, 1960.

New Catholic Encyclopedia. New York: McGraw-Hill Book Co.,
    1967.

Newman, John Henry. On Consulting the Faithful in Matters of
    Doctrine, edited and with an introduction by John Coulson.
    London: Geoffrey Chapman, 1961.

_____. The Via Media of the Anglican Church. London:
    Longmans, Green, 1895.

Nichols, James Hastings. Democracy and the Churches. Phila-
    delphia: Westminster Press, 1951.

_____. History of Christianity 1650-1950: Secu-
    larization of the West. New York: The Ronald Press, 1956.

Nielson, Fredrik. The History of the Papacy in the Nineteenth
    Century, trans. by A. J. Mason. 2 vols. London: J.
    Murray, 1906.

Nippold, Friedrich. The Papacy in the Nineteenth Century. New
    York: G. P. Putnam's Sons, 1900.

Novak, Michael. The Open Church. New York: The Macmillan
    Company, 1964.

O'Brien, Elmer, ed., Theology in Transition. New York: Herder&
    Herder, 1965.

Palmieri, Domenico. Tractatus de Romano Pontifice. 2nd ed.
    Prati: Giachetti, Filii et Soc., 1891.

Passaglia, Carlo. De Conciliis oecumenicis, edited and with an
    introduction and notes by Heribert Schauf. Freiburg/Br.:
    Herder, 1961.

_____. De Ecclesia Christi. Ratisbone: G. J.
    Manz, 1853.

_____. De Praerogativis beati Petri. Ratisbone:
    G. J. Manz, 1850.

Perrone, Giovanni. Praelectiones Theologicae. Rome, 1835-42.
    Citations from revised ed., Paris: Gaume Fratres, 1856.

Perrotta, Antonio. The Modernist Movement in Italy and Its
    Relation to the Spread of Protestant Christianity.
    Boston: The Gorham Press, 1929.

Petre, M. D. Alfred Loisy: His Religious Significance. Cam-
    bridge: The University Press, 1944.

ᅠ

ᅠ

ᅠ

_____. Modernism: Its Failure and Its Fruits. London: T. C. & E. C. Jack, 1918.

Polanyi, Michael. The Tacit Dimension. Garden City, New York: Doubleday & Company, Inc., 1966.

Popper, Karl. R. The Open Society and Its Enemies. London: G. Routledge and Sons, 1945.

Rahner, Karl. Theological Investigations, VI, trans. by Karl H. and Boniface Kruger. Baltimore: Helicon Press, 1969.

_____ and Joseph Ratzinger. Revelation and Tradition. New York: Herder & Herder, 1966.

_____. et al. Obedience and the Church. Washington: Corpus Books, 1968.

Ramsey, Ian T. Models and Mystery. London: Oxford University Press, 1964.

Ranchetti, Michele. The Catholic Modernists, trans. by Isabel Quigly. London: Oxford University Press, 1969.

Ratté, John. Three Modernists: Alfred Loisy, George Tyrrell and William L. Sullivan. New York: Sheed & Ward, 1967.

Rivière, Jean. Le Modernism dans l'Église, Étude d'Histoire Religieuse Contemporaine. Paris: Letouzey et Ane, 1929.

de Ruggiero, Guido. The History of European Liberalism. London: Oxford University Press, 1927.

Schauf, Heribert. Carlo Passaglia und Clemens Schrader, Beitrag zur Theolog geschichte des neunzehnten Jahrhundrets. Rome: Pontificia Universitas Gregoriana, 1938.

_____. De Corpore Christi Mystico sive de Ecclesia Christi theses. Die Ekklesiologie des Konzilstheologen Clemens Schrader, S.J. Freiburg: Herder, 1959.

_____. Die Einwohnung des Heiligen Geistes. Freiburg/Br.: Herder, 1941.

Scheeben, Matthias Joseph. The Mysteries of Christianity, trans. by Cyril Vollet. St. Louis: B. Herder Book Co., 1946.

Schmaus, Michael, ed., Die mündliche Überlieferung. Munich: Hueber, 1957.

Schnackenburg, Rudolph. The Church in the New Testament. London: Burns & Oates, 1965.

Schrader, Clemens. De theologico testium fonte. Paris: Lethielleux, 1878.

_____. De unitate Romana. Freiburg/Br.: Herder, 1862.

Shoof, T. Mark. A Survey of Catholic Theology: 1800-1970, trans. by N. D. Smith. Glen Rock: The Paulist Press, 1970.

184

Shook, Louis K., ed., Theology of Renewal. Montreal: Palm
    Publishers, 1968.

Simon, Yves. A General Theory of Authority. Notre Dame, India-
    na: University of Notre Dame Press, 1962.

Simpson, William J. S. Religious Thought in France in the Nine-
    teenth Century. London: G. Allen and Unwin, Ltd., 1935.

_____. Roman Catholic Opposition to Papal In-
    fallibility. London: John Murray, 1909.

Sullivan, Francis H. De Ecclesia: Quaestiones Theologiae
    Fundamentalis. Rome: Gregorian University Press, 1965.

Tavard, George H. Holy Writ or Holy Church. London: Burns &
    Oates, 1959.

_____. The Pilgrim Church. New York: Herder &
    Herder, 1967.

Tierney, Brian. Foundations of Conciliar Theory. Cambridge:
    The University Press, 1955.

Todd, John M., ed., Problems of Authority. Baltimore: Helicon
    Press, 1962.

Tromp, Sebastian. Actio catholica in corpore Christi. Rome:
    Gregorian University Press, 1936.

_____. Corpus Christi quod est Ecclesia,
    trans. by Ann Condit. New York: Vantage Press, 1960.

_____. Textus et documenta litterae encycli-
    cae De Mystico Jesu Christi Corpore. "Mystici Corporis
    Christ," Series Theologica 26. Rome: Gregorian University
    Press, 1948.

Tyrrell, George. Christianity at the Crossroads. London:
    Longmans, Green and Co., 1910.

_____. Medievalism: A Reply to Cardinal
    Mercier. London: Longmans, Green, and Co., 1909.

_____. The Programme of Modernism. New York:
    G. P. Putnam's Sons, 1908.

_____. Through Scylla and Charybdis. London:
    Longmans, Green, and Co., 1907.

Valeske, Ulrich. Votum Ecclesiae. Das Ringen um die Kirche
    in der neueren romisch-katholischen Theologie. Munich:
    Claudius Verlag, 1962.

Van den Eynde, Damien. Les Normes de l'enseignement chrétien
    dans la littérature patristique des trois premier siècles.
    Paris: Gembloux, 1933.

Vidler, Alec R. 20th Century Defenders of the Faith. London:
    SCM Press, Ltd., 1965.

_____. The Modernist Movement in the Roman
Church. Cambridge: The University Press, 1934.

_____. Prophecy and Papacy. New York: Scribner,
1954.

_____. A Variety of Catholic Modernists. Cam-
bridge: The University Press, 1970.

Walgrave, Jan-Henricus. Newman The Theologian, trans. by A. V.
Littledale. New York: Sheed & Ward, 1960.

Williamson, Benedict. The Treaty of the Lateran. London:
Burns Oates & Washbourne, Ltd., 1929.

Zapelena, Timotheus. De Ecclesia Christi. 2 vols. 6th ed.
Rome: Gregorian University Press, 1954-55.

Articles

Aubert, R. "La Geographie Ecclesiologique au XIXe Siècle."
Rev. Sc. Rel., 1960, pp. 11-56.

Bainvel, J. "Tradition and Living Magisterium." The Catholic
Encyclopedia, Vol. XV, 1912, pp. 6 ff.

Bartz, W. "Le Magistere de l'Église d'apres Scheeben." Rev.
Sc. Rel. XLVIII (1960), 309-28.

Baum, Gregory, "Infallibility Beyond Polemics." Commonweal,
XCIV, 5 (April 9, 1971), 103-05.

_____. "The Problem of the Magisterium Today"
(1), and "Toward a Renewed Theology of the Magisterium"
(II). IDOC Concilium, LXVII, 30-33.

Baum, Gregory. "Theology and Ideology." The Ecumenist,
January-February, 1970, pp. 25-31.

Baumgartner, C. "Tradition et Magistère." Rech. Sc. Rel., XLI
(1953). 161-89.

Benard, Edmund. "The Doctrinal Value of the Ordinary Teaching
of the Holy Father in View of Humani Generis." Proceedings of the 16th Annual Convention of the CTSA, pp. 78-
107.

Benoit, Pierre. "Inspiration et Revelation." Concilium, X
(1965), 13-26.

Bévenot, M. "Tradition, Church and Dogma." Heythrop Journal,
January, 1960, pp. 34-47.

Burghardt, W. J. "The Catholic Concept of Tradition in the
Light of Modern Theological Thought." Proceedings of the
6th Annual Convention of the CTSA, 1951.

Byrne, James J. "The Notion of Doctrinal Development in the
Anglican Writing of J. H. Newman." Ephemerides theologicae Lovanienses, XIV (1937), 230-86.

186

Ciappi, Louis. "Crisis of the Magisterium, Crisis of Faith?"
The Thomist, XXXII (1968), 147-70.

Colombo, Carlo Card. "Obedience to the Ordinary Magisterium."
Obedience and the Church. Washington: Corpus Books, 1968,
pp. 75-93.

Congar, Yves, M.-J. "Le Peuple Fidèle et la Fonction Prophetique de l'Église." Irenikon, XXIV (1951), 289-312 and
440-466.

Courtade, G. "J.-B. Franzelin, les Formules que le Magistère de
l'Église lui a Empruntees." Rec. Sc. Rel., XL (1951-52),
317-25.

Dejaifve, Gustave. "Bible, Tradition, Magistère dans la Theologie Catholique." Nouvelle Revue Theologie, LXXVIII
(1956), 135-51.

Donlon, S. E. "Authority, Ecclesiastical." National Catholic
Encyclopedia, I, 1115.

Draguet, R. "Book Review of Deneffe's Der Traditionsbegriff."
Emph. Theol. Lovan, IX (1932), 93-95.

Dulles, Avery. "The Contemporary Magisterium." Theology Digest,
XVII, 4 (Winter, 1969), 299-311.

Easton, David. "The New Revolution in Political Science." The
American Political Science Review, LXIII, 4 (December,
1969), 1051-61.

Fenton, Joseph. "The 'Humani Generis' and the Holy Father's
Ordinary Magisterium." Amer. Eccl. Rev., CXXV (1951),
53-62.

Filograssi, G. "Tradizione Divino-Apostolicae Magisterio della
Chiesa." Greg. XXXIII (1952), 135-67.

Heenan, John Cardinal. "The Authority of the Church." The
Tablet (London), CCXXII (May 18, 1968), 488.

Hill, Edmund. "Authority in the Church, Part I, In the N.T."
Clergy Review, L (1965), 619-28. Part II, Development of
Institutions, 674-85.

Iturrioz, P. Daniel. "De Traditione, Revelationis fonte, apud
theologos Societatis Jesu." De Scriptura et Traditione.
Rome: Pontificia Academia Mariana Internationalis, 1963,
pp. 397-429.

Kasper, Walter. "The Church Under the Word of God." Concilium,
IV (1965), 87-93.

Kerkvoorde, A. "La Formation Théologique de M.-J. Scheeben à
Rome." Ephm. theo. Lovan, XXII (1946), 174-93.

Lebreton, Jules. "Son Eminence Card. Billot." Etudes, CXXIX
(1911), 514-25.

Lynch, T., ed., "The Newman-Perrone Paper on Development."
Greg., XVI (1935), 402-47.

McCormick, Richard J. "The Magisterium and the Theologians."
Proceedings of the Catholic Theological Society of
America, XXIV (1969), 239-54.

_____. "Notes on Moral Theology." Theological
Studies, XXX, 4 (December, 1969), 635-44.

Rahner, Karl. "A Century of Infallibility." Theology Digest,
XVIII, 3 (Autumn, 1970), 216-21.

_____. The Historical Dimension in Theology."
Theology Digest, Sesquicentennial Issue (February, 1968),
pp. 30-42.

Rahner, Karl. "Philosophy and Philosophizing in Theology."
Theology Digest, Sesquicentennial Issue (February, 1968),
pp. 17-29.

_____. "Theology and the Magisterium after the
Council." Theology Digest, Sesquicentennial Issue
(February, 1968), pp. 4-16.

Van Rijn, I. "A Dutch View of Authority." America, March 23,
1968, pp. 371-74.

Shapere, Dudley. "Meaning and Scientific Change." Mind and
Cosmos: Essays in Contemporary Science and Philosophy.
Pittsburgh: The University Press, 1966, pp. 41-85.

_____. "The Structure of Scientific Revolution:
A Review." The Philosophical Review, LXXIII (1964), 383-
94.

Stanley, David M. "Authority in the Church: A New Testament
Reality." Catholic Biblical Quarterly, XXIX (1967), 555-
73.

Tavard, G. "Tradition in Early Post-Tridentine Theology."
Theological Studies, XXIII (1962), 377-405.

Tracy, David. "Review of Infallible? An Inquiry by Hans
Küng." The Christian Century, May 19, 1971, pp. 631-33.

da Viega, Coutinho, L. "Tradition et Histoire dans la con-
troverse moderniste (1898-1910)." Analecta Gregoriana,
LXXIII (1954).

Weiler, August. "Church Authority and Government in the
Middle Ages." Concilium, VII. Glen Rock: Paulist
Press, 1965.

Wolin, Sheldon S. "Political Theory as a Vocation." The
American Political Science Review, LXIII, 4 (December,
1969), 1062-82.